Qualitysense

Qualitysense

Organizational Approaches to Improving Product Quality and Service

Martin R. Smith

 a Division of
American Management Associations

Library of Congress Cataloging in Publication Data

Smith, Martin R   1934–
  Qualitysense.

  Includes index.
  1. Quality assurance. I. Title.
TS156.6.S54   658.5'62   79-18139
ISBN 0-8144-5534-4

FIRST PRINTING

This book is dedicated to the following men, and to others like them, who are pioneering the quality principles described in this book:

ROBERT J. BUCKLEY
Chairman and President, Allegheny Ludlum Industries, Inc.

JOHN A. DAVIDSON
Chairman, Harley-Davidson Motor Co., Inc.

THOMAS KROEHLE
Chief Executive Officer, Lee-Norse Division of Ingersoll-Rand Co.

NICHOLAS BABICH
President, Plastics Machinery Division, Leesona Corp.

Foreword

We have today in the United States a single, overriding problem in our economic system: inflation. From the President's Office to the offices of the many executives who run the thousands of companies in the United States, we are concerned with the fact that we are spending more than we are producing. This trend, which has been gaining momentum since the mid-sixties, has received serious attention only sporadically.

Some business people are quick to point out the underlying effect of government action as the cause of inflation. When our government spends more than it takes in, it has only one instrument in hand, that is, simply to inflate the currency. While this would seem amenable to solution, we have floundered miserably in attempting to come to consensus regarding the political action necessary.

Perhaps it is wrong to concentrate on government spending, because we may be led to believe that there is nothing else to be done but to reverse the action of government. There are other causes, and they may not get the emphasis they deserve. I refer to a long-term trend in American manufacturing—namely, the growing reduction of worker productivity in most of our manufacturing industries. In a typical American company, statistics show that gains in productivity are largely attributable to investment in labor-saving tools and processes. Despite the fact that the backbreaking labor associated with the manufacturing industries at the dawn of the Industrial Revolution has disappeared, the ability of the individual worker to improve his personal productivity has declined.

Coupled with this trend is the fact that much of the so-called consumerism problem is associated with a perception of the *quality* of the products offered the public. Perhaps there is an unreasonable preoccupation with defects in the complex machines we build and sell to the public. On the other hand, perhaps we are not utilizing all our skills or ingenuity to get the quality we can.

Martin Smith, in his book *Qualitysense,* thoroughly examines the issue of quality in manufacturing, and collects striking examples of our failure to attain it. This extremely well-written, well-organized, and down-to-earth book should be required reading not only for the top management of any company genuinely concerned with improving its quality but for all the functional managers of the business as well. Mr. Smith examines with a cutting incisiveness the way we go after quality and, after pointing out all that is wrong with our approach, lays out the solutions.

Smith uses the dramatic example of the transition of the Quasar TV manufacturing company from American to Japanese management in the United States. He calls it "The Quasar Humiliation," and the simple lesson he so vividly describes is that, with a simple change in the attitude and attention given the problems of quality, Quasar realized incredible gains in productivity for the company. The Japanese managers of the company would simply not accept the same standards the American managers had grown used to.

He describes the ten deadly sins of quality assurance most of us find all too familiar from our own experience. At the heart of this book is his examination of the attitude of individuals and companies. We have undeniably decided that quality is an expense, and the way to reduce it is to reduce the level of attention we give it or the expense that would be necessary to attain it. Smith rightfully directs our attention to the fact that in many cases we have pushed quality control down to the lowest possible denominator, typically where only a narrow band of people can have any input. Why, for example, do we place quality control in manufacturing functions where, because of traditional functional barriers, it can have little or no influence on design? By doing so, we doom ourselves to correcting defects instead of preventing them.

The logic is obvious. Why have we spent so much time trying not to understand it? One reason is that in the recent past quality control has relied more and more on the technical aspect of statistics and other analytical methods. We have forgotten how important the attitude and the influence of the individual are. Smith calls attention at one point to the fact that we encourage the technical staff in quality control to participate in seminars. These seminars teach the new tools or implement measurement technique almost as though the quality control staff will be able to correct the errors of the hundreds of people who directly influence the product.

Furthermore, the technical expertise gained by an elite group of supervisory people often serves only to separate that group from those who are genuinely at the root of the problem. Smith admonishes us to realize that quality is achievable within business limits and that businessmen need only act as businessmen to improve the quality of their products.

Qualitysense is really a fine book. It teaches; it exposes; and it proposes constructive solutions. It is absolutely down to earth and strikes at the heart of the matter. Without equivocation, it is recommended to today's management.

> *Robert J. Buckley*
> Chairman and President
> Allegheny Ludlum Industries, Inc.

Preface

Something must be done to improve quality. Before it can get better, however, we must first understand that it is getting worse. Too many people today are playing ostrich, sticking their heads in the sand, avoiding the unpleasant truth that, for a number of reasons, product and service quality are deteriorating.

Unless *we* do something about it, quality will continue to slide backward. You (whatever your job title) and I are the people who must make things better. We are the doctors and the patient is quality. If we as executives, supervisors, administrators, teachers, and quality assurance professionals don't take the right remedial action, the patient will get worse, and possibly die.

But before we cure the patient, we must educate the doctor. The doctor must open his eyes to the fact that his diagnostic skills are lacking; that his curative powers are not being appropriately used. And that is the purpose of Chapter I—to illustrate, in somewhat dramatic terms, how easy it is to abandon common sense and good judgment and opt for the difficult and wrong solutions.

After we face the fact that many quality programs are on the wrong track because of misconceptions and poor judgment, we go on to the next step. In Chapter II we expose many of the poor quality practices that have given quality assurance a bad reputation and hurt its chances for success. The final chapters of this book explore and recommend practices to improve product and support quality.

Chapters III and IV deal specifically, although not exclusively, with ways and means of implementing a successful quality program for most companies. They explain various techniques and practices that have helped upgrade quality levels for many different industries.

The cornerstone of professionalism in any job is the ability to relate its function to other functions of the business in order to get the job done. Quality assurance is certainly no exception. The way it goes about doing things, the manner in which it works with people from other functions, the contributions it makes to company (not just quality) goals, marks quality assurance either as a contributor or as a dud. It is of the greatest importance to every quality practitioner that he or she learn how to professionalize his or her activity. Chapter V is dedicated to teaching the necessary skills to the quality practitioner.

Chapter VI tests your skills—what you have learned by reading this book. Then it takes a peek at the future directions of quality.

Martin R. Smith

Contents

Chapter I

How Effective Are Your Quality Skills?

Everybody is ignorant, only on different subjects.
—WILL ROGERS

1. The Quasar Humiliation

In a small town in Illinois in 1974 Quasar Electronic Company, a part of the Matsushita Electronic Industrial Company of Japan, acquired a faltering U.S. television operation and formed Quasar Electronics Company, U.S.A. In the intervening three years Quasar completely turned the operation around. In the American television industry the average defect rate is about 150 defects (total accumulated defects throughout the entire production cycle) for every 100 TV sets built. Quasar's average defect rate is now 15 defects for every 100 sets, a factor *ten times better than the American average.* By comparison, a sister Quasar facility in Japan operates at one-half defect for every 100 sets.

There was a time when discussions about Japanese quality could elicit a chuckle at any quality gathering. Their product quality was notoriously poor and variable. Any product bought from Japanese manufacturers was almost destined to be shoddy. Today that situation has been totally reversed. Japanese quality is among the very best in the world. When you purchase a Japanese product you can almost always count on its performance and reliability.

In fact, the Japanese have taught some lessons to their former teachers—the Americans—about quality. In one sense the quality levels Quasar has achieved have far surpassed anything experienced by its U.S. counterparts. Quasar, in effect, has humiliated many American companies.

What, then, has gone wrong? Why hasn't American quality kept pace with the Japanese? Why this sense of uneasiness about the ability of our products to meet the expectations of consumers? And why are we experiencing such a variety of product and service quality problems, including car recalls, adulterated drugs, toys that harm children, and inadequate medical care?

Much has been written about the state of the art of U.S. product quality, and many reasons have been given to explain the difficulties. Yet none really appears to drive to the core of the problem; the explanations are superficial. The argument that American craftsmen leave something to be desired, for example, is advanced as the prime cause for a variety of sins ranging from low productivity to shoddy quality. Yet we all know that, apart from a small percentage of people either unwilling or unable to do good work, the overwhelming number of American craftsmen want to do a good job, and will do so provided they are properly motivated and directed. The Americans working at Quasar are an example. The same workmen were present before the turnaround engineered by Quasar. The desire to do worthwhile work is an innate characteristic, common to working people the world over.

Rampant unionism has been called a devastating force with an onerous influence on product quality. Unionism, it is claimed, destroys workers' incentive. If that is the case, why is German quality so outstanding? German unions are among the most powerful in the world. Another fact to consider: for the past 20 years American union membership has been declining. Product quality, during that same period, has experienced its share of problems. If the argument that unionism has a deleterious effect on product quality were true, the decline in union membership should have triggered an improvement in quality levels. But that does not appear to have happened.

Some advance the proposition that quality levels have held steady at acceptable levels over the years. They argue that the only radical change has been the steadily increasing sophistication of consumers; that these consumers are no longer satisfied with the level of quality they once considered acceptable. There is much to be said for that proposition. Consumers are more sophisticated nowadays and they are demanding better quality than ever before. But these demands are a reality of the marketplace; they form a condition of product acceptance. They are not a *cause* of quality problems. That's putting the cart before the horse. Consumers are demanding better quality, and companies must accept that condition and gear their quality efforts to customer expectations.

To understand why we cannot satisfy consumers and why we face substantial quality problems today it is first necessary to recognize that quality assurance has traditionally been viewed as a technical function with roots in the manufacturing process. When manufacturing progressed from the era of the individual craftsman to the era of mass production, the responsibility for quality was passed from the worker producing the goods to an inspector who could read blueprints and who understood how to interpret product and process specifications. The inspector's orientation was essentially technical; he was required to have a working knowledge of the manufacturing process and a rudimentary knowledge of gauging and measurement techniques.

When the inspection function broadened into quality assurance the manager, or chief inspector, as he was most commonly known, was awarded his job because he had gained more technical insight than any other inspector. His technical orientation remained unchanged and unchallenged.

Then the era of statistics blossomed. The science of the measurement and interpretation of variability in the manufacturing process became a major tool of quality assurance practitioners. It spread like wildfire and soon became *the* predominant technique in quality assurance, so much so, in fact, that it excluded many other productive and worthwhile techniques. Statistics became the messiah of quality assurance.

The burning desire to use statistics as a panacea for all quality problems still captivates many quality assurance practitioners. By now that desire has been supplemented and expanded by the love affair quality assurance is having with the new "systems" approach and by high technology. Too many quality assurance practitioners today don't consider themselves professionals unless they have mastered the latest systems innovation, the most up-to-date statistical method (experimental design is currently in vogue), and the newest advance in technology. Most dangerous of all, they don't really feel content until they have installed the newest device in their operations—whether or not it is needed, and whether or not it can do the job.

We can learn something very instructive from the Quasar humiliation. The Japanese have obviously mastered quality assurance. Their high-quality levels attest to that. *The Japanese have learned how to work with fundamentals to achieve a quality product.* The Quasar example abounds with lessons in simplicity. The following is a partial list of what Quasar did when it took over the American television plant in 1974:

1. Did a thorough life-cycle testing of product components.
2. Used a pilot line to plan production.
3. Made a detailed description of the process and detailed instructions of what to do and how to do it for all operators.
4. Did a predesign of work stations to minimize chances of operator error.
5. Separated lines containing similar parts.
6. Screened critical components before assembly.

Notice that there was no attempt to use complex statistical sampling plans; nor was there any evident compulsion to "systematize." Rather, the Japanese applied some very basic commonsense quality assurance techniques and those techniques have worked, and worked splendidly.

Now we arrive at the core of our quality problems: *We haven't learned how to keep things simple.* We exhibit a compulsive urge to complicate matters, and that compulsion has forced us to shunt aside the productive quality techniques that are so desperately needed to improve product and service quality.

As a corollary to the above statement, *top management has too often failed to recognize the profitmaking potential of quality assurance.* Treating it as a strictly technical function has caused it to respond only as a technical function. If its potential is realized, quality assurance can make significant contributions to profits and sales.

And that's what the rest of this book is about. It's called qualitysense, and it can be defined as a workable marriage between commonsense principles on the one hand, and some fundamental quality assurance techniques on the other hand. A fertile joining will yield quality programs of high effectiveness. As you read along, this theme will be developed fully. But for now, let's move forward and test *your* qualitysense.

2. How Good Is Your Qualitysense?

Let's test your qualitysense skills. This is the perfect opportunity to do so. Chances are that you're by yourself, with nobody peeking over your shoulder. Consequently, you are relaxed and under no pressure to look good in somebody else's eyes. So this test is best taken right now when you can not only answer every question to the best of your ability, but also evaluate the test results without fear of your supervisor or anybody else criticizing any of your responses.

It is important that you take this test before you read the book. Only in this way can the theme of the book impact and register. It will help you focus clearly on the significance of every subsequent topic. More importantly, it will clear the smoke and allow you to analyze each subject objectively for yourself without the prejudice of past experience interfering with the proper solution.

The problems presented here are universal. Be honest with yourself and answer every problem just as if you were directly involved in each case and a great deal depended on the correct answer. Answer *all* six problems before you read the answers.

Ready? Then let's start.

Problem #1: The Sagging Reputation of Quality Assurance

You have recently been hired as quality manager by a company that has been experiencing severe quality problems. Quality problems abound with products in customers' hands, scrap and rework costs are sky-high, and cost of quality is out of sight. People in manufacturing, engineering, marketing, and other departments have little or no respect for the abilities of the quality assurance department, and look down their noses at its members. Quality assurance supervisors have the overall reputation of being ineffective and generally ridiculous. Few employees desire to work with or associate with quality people in this company.

Your job is to restore the reputation of quality assurance and get the company's quality program back on track. The way you see it, your first job is to upgrade the quality assurance organization and install practices to gain the respect of other people in the company. Your best strategy is to:

1. Fire most of the existing quality assurance supervisors and staff the department with technically oriented quality assurance people.
2. Insist on strict adherence to established company standards and engineering specifications.
3. Send quality assurance supervisors and inspectors to training schools to improve their technical abilities.
4. All of the above.
5. Establish a quality plan that focuses on company return-on-investment goals.
6. None of the above.

Problem #2: Those Nagging Quality Problems

You are president of a growing, family-held bicycle manufacturing concern. This year your firm captured 10 percent of the market and placed sixth in the rankings by total sales of all bicycle manufacturers in the country. You have ambitious plans for the future and hope to have 30 percent of the market within five years. To do that you have budgeted monies for both plant expansion and acquisitions, and you are in the process of hiring capable people to assist with the plans.

The only major problem that could restrict sales is quality. For the past several years the quality of your product has been slipping, and the quality image you have tried so desperately to maintain is rapidly deteriorating. Problems have erupted with design, manufacture, materials, and field service. The whole business structure appears to be crumbling.

The worst of the company's quality problems occurred six months ago when about 200 customer complaints were received about front wheel forks breaking. Unfortunately, when this happens and the bicycle is in motion, the front wheel falls off. So far lawsuits and the cost of repairing the defective bicycles and of recalling several hundred more bicycles with the suspected defect have added up to a cost to the company of $175,000. For a small manufacturer this represents a prodigious quantity of dollars.

Your quality assurance organization is incapable of coping with the magnitude and type of problems experienced. Rather than expanding its capabilities in line with company growth, quality assurance is still living in the past when a few hundred bicycles were assembled weekly instead of the thousands weekly that are put out now.

You know you must do something, but you are not sure what you should do. So you plan to have quality assurance operations analyzed for your company before you make any move. Your problem is to decide which approach will yield the best method. These are the alternatives:

1. Have marketing analyze customer quality failures, and manufacturing and engineering do the same. Then sit down with the respective managers and organize an improvement program.
2. Contract a prestigious consulting firm to make a study and suggest recommendations for improvement.
3. Hire a top-caliber quality assurance professional to run and improve the quality assurance organization.
4. Contract a one-man quality assurance consultant to analyze the operations and make recommendations.
5. Have your industrial engineering department analyze the operations and make recommendations for improvements.

Which one would you select?

Problem #3: Bad News City

You've got a bone-crushing problem to contend with. Your company manufactures widgets, and during the last three months four consumers have been seriously injured using your product. A recent design change, introduced to cost reduce the widget, has caused unexpected changes in the product, resulting in damage to users. You are quality assurance manager for your company, and you approved the design change along with the president, vice-president of product engineering, and other department heads. Although none of you realized the recent design change made the widgets dangerous to use, all of you were aware of the *potential* for injury. You simply and honestly thought the probabilities of injury were remote. The question is: what is your liability?

1. You can go to jail.
2. You can personally lose a civil suit and be assessed damages.
3. You can lose your job and damage your professional reputation.
4. All of the above.
5. None of the above.
6. Since you work for a corporation, recognized not as any individual person but as an entity under the law, nothing serious can happen to you. You are protected by the "umbrella" of the corporation.

Problem #4: Those Scrap and Rework Blues

Your company is confronted with constantly increasing scrap and rework costs. As general manager of the company it is your responsibility to reduce those costs so the profit plan can be made. Without scrap and rework reductions you won't be able to cut costs. You have several possibilities to consider:

1. Add inspectors to high-cost areas of the manufacturing process.

2. Give scrap and rework cost responsibility to manufacturing; take it away from quality assurance.
3. Have the quality assurance manager start a statistical quality control program.
4. Begin a motivation campaign to try to instill pride in the manufacturing organization.
5. Hang quality banners around the plant and make speeches convincing everyone of your sincerity in reducing scrap and rework.
6. All of the above.
7. None of the above.

Problem #5: Your Friendly Vendors

Vendor quality problems have been plaguing your business. Defective parts and materials from vendor plants have been creating downtime and escalating rework costs, not to mention missed customer delivery dates of your products. As purchasing manager you confer with the quality assurance manager to decide on a course of action. Several options are available to you. Which would you choose?

1. Start a vendor rating system.
2. Begin source inspection at vendors' plants.
3. Add more inspectors to the receiving function.
4. Notify vendors you are assuming they have a capable quality system; then make them step up to their responsibilities.
5. Call in all your vendors and have a vendor quality conference.

Problem #6: The Troubled Quality Engineer

You are a quality engineering supervisor for a medium-sized independent testing laboratory that has been growing at a fairly rapid rate for the past several years. Although next year's growth forecast doesn't look as good as it has for the last few years, you are confident that the long-term forecast is rosy, and this confidence is shared by company management.

You are at that somewhat troubled phase when your company is beginning its metamorphosis from a small to a large company with all the concomitant problems that poses. Your department has managed astutely to keep pace with the changes, although you are stuck with a great many headaches attributable to growth.

One of those small but nagging problems involves the new laser-beam testing department you proposed and then helped establish two years ago. From an initial installation of three special laser testers, you are up to five, and you plan to add two more next year. Start-up costs have generally been absorbed at this stage, and the company is beginning to show a small profit from the operation.

The problem, however, is that the company that built the testing machines has been servicing them without charge. However, when you contracted to buy the machines, nobody, not even the manufacturer, anticipated the amount of service they would require. Since these are costly pieces of equipment, it is essential this service be provided to keep the testing machines running. Otherwise, downtime costs will eat up the department's tiny profit margin.

You have several alternatives available. The trouble is selecting the one that would be most beneficial to the department.

1. Go see the general manager of the company that built the testing machines and tell him you will cancel the orders for the two new machines unless he can provide the services needed.
2. Train an engineer from another department to service the equipment.

3. Hire an engineer to service the equipment.
4. Contract an outside engineering firm to service the equipment.
5. Do nothing and wait to see what happens.

What would *you* do?

Answer to Problem #1: The Sagging Reputation of Quality Assurance

One of the worst things you could do as the new quality assurance manager is to fire your staff and hire technical people. That's probably what got the company into trouble to begin with. You're most certainly just replacing one technically oriented group with another. The real problem with quality assurance today is that it concentrates too heavily on technical achievement but does little to plan the quality program as a business activity that meshes with the company's profit plans.

If you select the second choice and insist on strict adherence to company specifications and standards, you haven't contributed anything. That just doesn't solve problems. Not that you shouldn't adhere to specifications; obviously you must. Specifications are the documents that guide manufacture of the product. But cracking the whip over production doesn't solve the problems; changing and improving the specifications probably will. Chances are if you do the former you will only be looked upon as a purist.

Sending your supervisors and inspectors to training school is only skirting the problem. There is no correlation between the efficiency of inspectors and reduced quality problems. If anything, the trained inspectors will find *more* problems for you to contend with.

The correct answer is to establish a quality plan that focuses on company return-on-investment (ROI) goals. Making up the plan will automatically force you to think through the problems and the approaches necessary to resolve those problems. Sections 4 and 5 of Chapter III will spell out specifics on how to accomplish your goals.

The whole premise of this book is that quality practitioners have somehow stumbled onto the wrong path in their search for better quality. They have adopted the mantle of technical sophistication as their chief protector against proliferating quality problems, and they are suffering for it. In a well-balanced quality program, technical sophistication is reduced to its proper role—it becomes an element of the quality plan, not the plan itself. For quality to improve, quality practitioners must install *total quality systems* for all functions of the company. This subject is explained in Chapter III.

Answer to Problem #2: Those Nagging Quality Problems

If you select alternative 1, your results will be marginal at best. After all, your current organization got you into trouble to begin with. Chances are the same basic mistakes it has been making will be perpetuated. It's reasonable to assume that the company's inability to cope with the problem won't really change just because you discuss it with the managers.

The same general line of reasoning holds true for alternative 5. Although industrial engineers are trained to ferret out inefficiencies, they have been exposed to these particular quality problems for so long their viewpoints on how to improve quality may be stagnant. This latter conclusion implies the need for outside involvement.

Now what do you do? Use a one-man consultant; engage a large, prestigious consulting firm; or hire a quality assurance professional?

If you hire the quality assurance professional before the study is made, you have put the cart before the horse. A thorough study may reveal that the current organization is geared to handle the problem with a few shifts in organizational responsibility coupled with some quality assurance training for selected employees. Why pay for a high-priced pro unless you are convinced you need him? And is it prudent to do that without first charting the course of quality in the company over the next five years or so? Naturally, to make such an extended plan necessitates an analysis of current and projected problems and opportunities. Therefore, a study of quality becomes the first order of business.

Do you contract for the services of the large firm or the consultant who works for himself? Obviously both types of professional consultants have the necessary objectivity to do a good job because they are not a part of your company. They also have a storehouse of experience from having solved similar problems for many other companies.

Chances are the big firm, which has a large overhead, will be more expensive when contrasted to the private consultant who operates out of a suitcase. This doesn't mean the quality of the work is proportionate to the size of the firm. On the contrary. It has been my experience that the private consultant will often do a better job. One reason is that he has done the same type of job many times over. Although that total experience is present in the big consulting firm, it is more diffused. The consultant who does a good job is soon promoted and moved out, and a new man is brought in. For you, that means the experience level of the consultant doing the job in your company is usually considerably less than that of the consultant who works for himself. It does make a difference.

When the job is completed the large firm will present you with a beautiful leather-tooled manual containing its recommendations. The self-employed consultant doesn't have the money to commit to frills. What he will do, however, is make recommendations, then stay on the job and help you implement them. He will also arrive at those recommendations sooner than the large company (which must look at total billing dollars to cover its overhead) and install them more quickly.

It is to your advantage, in this case, to opt for the self-employed consultant.

Answer to Problem #3: Bad News City

Forget answer 6, "Since you work for a corporation, recognized not as any individual person but as an entity under the law, nothing serious can happen to you. You are protected by the 'umbrella' of the corporation." That kind of protection may have helped you in prior years, but it has totally vanished from today's courts of law across the country.

Today any person in any corporation can be held responsible for individual acts that result in injury to people and damage to property. Nobody is immune. Even though you mean well, if you exercise poor judgment (a fairly common mistake) regarding a decision that can be tied in with injury to consumers, you just might find yourself being assessed damages. The grounds are that, as a practicing quality professional, you failed to live up to your responsibilities. Even worse, if you *knowingly* allow a potentially injurious product to be shipped to customers and serious injury does result, as in this particular example, you could end up in jail.

Nothing is more frightening, is it? That *you, personally,* could lose your assets, your job, and your career, and be treated by society as a common criminal is really too much to handle. But it could happen, and in many cases, it already has. The correct answer, therefore, is 4: "All of the above."

The trend of holding people, rather than impersonal institutions such as corporations, culpable looks as if it will continue. Every company officer, manager, engineer, and quality assurance manager (in particular) owes it to himself or herself to know what must be done for self-protection in case of a lawsuit. Section 9 in Chapter IV is a good starting point. It provides a beginning for learning how to establish a products liability program.

Answer to Problem #4: Those Scrap and Rework Blues

Adding inspectors to any operation anywhere does not solve quality problems. It only adds to quality costs and tends to perpetuate the problems, institutionalize them, and damn near make them respectable. Therefore, the first answer is wrong. Too many quality practitioners use this approach, and ineluctably they perish. It behooves every quality assurance manager to understand that inspectors, by their very nature, are after the fact. By definition, they can only screen the good from the bad; they do not eliminate the bad.

Many quality managers respond to high scrap and rework levels by installing the newest statistical technique. Section 4 in Chapter II, "Too Many Statistics, Not Enough Sense," deals with that problem adequately. It is enough to say here that statistical techniques are not universally appropriate; nor are they well understood by the manufacturing population at large. Statistics can help in individual situations, but experience has taught me that as a wholesale solution to problems, they usually don't work. That puts the skids under answer 3.

Answers 4 and 5 are similar. Banners, speeches, campaigns, publicity, and the like do not always produce the desired results. In fact, any favorable response is short-lived and tends to evaporate as soon as the speakers go home and the banners come down. In other words these represent superficial approaches. They may help dress up a quality cost reduction program, but they have no substance by themselves.

My experience and the experiences of many other quality professionals have taught us that the best results are obtained when we say:

Look, Mr. Manufacturing, scrap and rework is your responsibility. You control the manufacturing process, and your promotions and raises are based on performance. You are measured by delivery, safety, head count, and costs. Why shouldn't you be measured by quality? These are legitimate costs too, and unless you are made accountable for them you won't pay any attention to them. That's just human nature.

If you don't place as great a significance on quality as you do on other costs, the responsibility will pass to quality assurance. And we can't control your operation for you. Those are your operators, your tools, your materials, your equipment. They don't work for quality assurance. What we can do for you is to give you a quality system to help you control and measure the process. Beyond that we are ineffective.

Quality assurance does not design, manufacture, or market the product. Product engineers, manufacturing people, and marketing men and women do that. Until they understand that quality is *their job* and *their responsibility,* you won't get quality. The best, most effective quality assurance department has few inspectors, few supervisors, and few engineers. The lack of need for a large staff shows that the functional departments are living up to their responsibilities. A big quality assurance department is usually a sign that quality problems are abundant and quality costs high. It is a tip-off that quality assurance has been given the responsibility for doing jobs best handled by other people—a ploy that *never* works.

Answer 2 is the proper response.

Answer to Problem #5: Your Friendly Vendors

We have already covered the question of the effects of inspectors on problem resolution. So answer 3 is ruled out. Starting a vendor rating system, answer 1, is a good start but that's all it is. By itself it doesn't reduce vendor defects—it simply identifies them. So we can eliminate that answer.

Answer 2, source inspection, is more of the same after-the-fact approach. It doesn't resolve the problems; it simply adds inspection costs to them. It is even more expensive because you are adding travel costs to the inspection costs.

Calling the vendors in for a conference is a good way to meet some nice people, but doesn't answer any organizational objectives. As soon as the conference is over, the topic will fade from people's minds. Conferences are not a self-perpetuating mechanism for problem resolution.

The correct answer is 4. Notify your vendors to assure their quality system is capable of meeting your product specifications consistently, then make them live up to their contracts. Over the years I have found this to be the best approach. Tell them what you expect, make sure they are supplied with understandable specifications, assess their process (before the contract is signed), and then give them the green light.

Keep up-to-date records of their performance and notify them through purchasing when you reject material. Have them come back to you *in each case* and let you know what was done to correct the problem. If they continue to send lots of defective material call them into *your* plant (don't go to theirs; it's too expensive) and make sure they know what must be done to stop the problem. Don't solve the problem for them. Make that their responsibility. That's what you're paying them for. If they still supply defective material, find another vendor. (See Section 4 in Chapter IV.)

Answer to Problem #6: The Troubled Quality Engineer

The answer to this problem is not as easy as a superficial analysis would lead you to believe. Actually, the *real* problem isn't which alternative to select. If your thinking were geared to hard-core basics, the solution would be readily apparent. The problem, rather, is to be able to analyze the problem objectively without stereotyped thinking interfering with a proper analysis.

To most observers alternative 2, "Train an engineer from another department to service the equipment"; 3, "Hire an engineer to service the equipment"; or 4, "Contract an outside engineering firm to service the equipment" would provide the so-called "logical" solution.

However, there is only one prime answer—#1, "Go see the general manager of the company that built the testing machines and tell him you will cancel the orders for the two new machines unless he can provide the services needed."

Right now, you're probably wrinkling your nose in distaste. You ask yourself how any experienced manager, given this problem, could possibly arrive at such a horrendous conclusion. Well, let's analyze it together.

First, let's state the objectives of the new laser testing department: to grow in volume and profits. Then remember that the department is a two-year-old newcomer. Next, it is important to realize that during the early and formative years of a department, management closely scrutinizes operating results. Although management initially decided to go ahead with the operation there is *never* any firm commitment to support a loser indefinitely. Therefore, whatever must be done to get the laser testing department operational must be done during the first year or two, when start-up costs are anticipated and planned. After that it is important that the department show some promise of coming out of the red. Otherwise, management may justifiably rethink its position and move to cut costs by terminating or severely curtailing operations.

So it remains your responsibility (you proposed the operation in the first place) to maintain and expand that small and tenuous operating profit that is just beginning to be realized.

If you add another man to the budget or contract for outside services, you know your profit margin will be destroyed for the current year. And you really can't afford to let this happen, particularly since the amount of service required by the testing machines was not anticipated and, therefore, not planned for in the budget. Management doesn't particularly care whose fault that is. It just wants to see results, and it is holding *you* accountable.

Under those circumstances, you really have only one feasible alternative. Go to the manufacturer of the equipment and let him know that his mistake in missing the importance of the service requirement might not only cause the cancellation of the two testing machines he is now building for you, but could also result in the entire department being shut down to minimize losses.

He is almost certain to provide a full-time service technician—for even a year, if necessary. It would be cheaper for him than losing the next order for two testing machines, which he has already started manufacturing. Another factor he will surely consider is the loss of reputation he would suffer if it became known in the industry that he failed to provide the necessary help to get his specialized equipment in operation. He might even offer to reduce the price of the current and subsequent orders to help amortize the cost to you of providing the needed expertise if he doesn't have enough help available to service the equipment.

In either case, you have protected your department's profit margin (and, incidentally, your reputation). What you can do now is budget for the needed help when the manufacturer can no longer provide assistance—say a year or two down the road. By then the new department should be sufficiently in the black to absorb the extra expense and still attain planned profits.

Chapter II

Why Things Are
in Such a Mess

*The only things that evolve by themselves in an
organization are disorder, friction, and malper-
formance.*

—PETER DRUCKER

1. The Ten Deadly Sins of Quality Assurance

The ten deadly sins of quality assurance are

1. Too much attention to technical razzle-dazzle; not enough attention to profits, sales, and costs.
2. Too much time trying to stop defects; not enough time trying to prevent defects.
3. Too heavy a reliance on statistics; not enough reliance on good judgment.
4. Too much concentration on product specifications; not enough understanding of customers' needs.
5. Too much devotion to nit-picking; not enough attention to solving major quality problems.
6. Too much concentration on manufacturing; too little attention to quality of design and service.
7. Too much time in the office; not enough time on the firing line.
8. Too much technical education for quality assurance technicians; too little practical education of operators, draftsmen, servicemen, and others responsible for getting quality.
9. Too heavy a focus on quality levels; not enough devotion to quality cost reduction.
10. Too much time spent complaining about poor attitudes toward quality; not enough focus on motivating people and convincing them of the value of quality.

The capability of providing customers with top-quality products and top-quality services appears to be an elusive devil, hard to catch, and even harder to hold on to for many quality practitioners. Somehow, things seem to have gone wrong. Dissatisfied customers, poor service, high scrap costs, excessive warranty—all of these and more are plaguing management people in the quality assurance field.

In most cases, quality assurance people lay the blame on somebody else's doorstep. The management isn't interested in quality, it won't approve enough money for testing equipment, it won't allow for the hiring of a new quality engineer, quality assurance has no voice in new products approval, the marketing people ignore quality assurance, and so on. The list is seemingly endless.

Yet to some extent all this grumbling is justified. Many top managements have no real grasp of the profit potential of product quality, controllers automatically tighten purse strings when quality is mentioned, and product engineers and marketing people just don't want quality assurance people fumbling around their bailiwicks digging up skeletons.

But who is to blame? All those other managers, so righteously condemned by quality assurance for their lack of understanding, can only make judgments of quality assurance based on how they see quality assurance doing its job. If quality assurance people are doing the wrong things, or if they are behaving badly, who can be blamed for shunning them?

And therein lies the problem. Quality assurance has the wrong image. Too many businessmen think of quality assurance as a necessary evil. When they think of quality assurance practitioners their thoughts read like this: purists, do-gooders, policemen, narrow technical specialists, and second-rate managers.

Why does quality assurance have this shoddy image? Simply because much of the time businessmen have been right. Too many quality assurance people have deserved all the derogatory comments made above, and more. Let's dissect the basic criticisms—the ten deadly sins of quality assurance people—and discover very specifically why their reputations are suffering.

1. *Too much attention to technical razzle-dazzle; not enough attention to profits, sales, and costs.* Most quality assurance managers have a technical background, either in product engineering or in manufacturing engineering. They have viewed their function as a technical specialty and accordingly have stressed the technical aspects of their jobs. Statistics, gauge design, reliability models, product specifications, inspection methodology, prototype testing, and other related technical subjects have captured their attention to the exclusion of profits, sales, and costs. Their viewpoints have been restricted.

To some extent this failing can be blamed on top management. Viewed as an intricate technical specialty, quality assurance has been assigned to a lower management echelon similar to that for such other functional specialties as market research and tool design.

Quality assurance people are often reluctant to couple their efforts to results-producing activities. They fail to define the role of quality assurance in terms of company objectives. Rather, they allow the dazzle of technical expertise to blind them to the realities of business life. Because they feel more at home with technical matters than with broad-based business functions, they fail to evaluate their function in terms of dollars and cents and contribution to sales. They forget that the most sophisticated analytical method is only as good as its ability to get results in the most economical manner. In short, they blindfold themselves; the kind of product quality we get today attests to that conclusion.

2. *Too much time trying to stop defects; not enough time trying*

to prevent defects. One of the most devastating charges leveled at quality assurance is that it is more involved with stopping defects than with preventing them. Probably more than any other criticism, this one does the greatest damage to the reputation of quality assurance. And to a large extent it is true.

Not that quality assurance isn't *interested* in preventive methods. It is. (The exceptions are some ultrapurist quality assurance types who think of their function as keeping defects from leaving the factory, but not preventing them. One, just one, quality assurance manager of this type can cause irreversible damage to the reputation of quality assurance in a company for *years*.)

But quality assurance is often hampered in its efforts to achieve a true preventive-oriented quality effort simply because it doesn't know how to go about converting its function from the impotent policeman approach. Its technical orientation dominates its thinking. Again, the failure of quality assurance to think of its function as broad based stymies its efforts to do a better job. If cost-of-quality reporting is missing, for example, there is no way to measure results and the first essential ingredient of any improvement program is absent. Although cost of quality has become a standard, accepted part of the quality tool kit, many companies do not use it, even those companies with a reputation for sophistication in management systems. Chances are that if cost of quality isn't used, other techniques for the measurement and prevention of defects are also missing. That is not always the case, but I believe there is a high correlation.

3. *Too heavy a reliance on statistics; not enough reliance on good judgment.* It's almost as if quality assurance is afraid to rely on good judgment and rushes to statistics to take its place. Good judgment is, after all, the most subjective basis of decisionmaking. It is art rather than science. And quality

assurance is oriented toward science, not art. Most quality assurance practitioners have been trained in technical disciplines and understand how to react to factual data. But so much of the time either factual data are not available or too much time is needed to extract them when decisions are needed quickly. Therefore, subjective decisions need to be made from the limited amount of information available. Many quality assurance managers can't handle that. In tight situations they tend to resort to their sampling plans or experimental designs or tests for significance of differences. By the time all the data needed have been collected, it is too late. The time for a decision has come and gone. In effect, the decision has been taken from their hands.

4. *Too much concentration on product specifications; not enough understanding of customers' needs.* The same illusion of the efficacy of relying on statistics for answers to quality problems holds doubly true for product specifications. Too many quality assurance people would much prefer working with product specifications to talking to customers to gain an understanding of their needs.

But specifications have a tendency to drift away from specific customer needs when designs need to be modified to accommodate the manufacturing process or when cost reduction is essential. (A cheaper material might be substituted, for example, but it might result in a shorter product life.)

It is axiomatic that the very livelihood of quality assurance depends on customer acceptance of the product. If customers are satisfied with their purchases and find little wrong with them, quality assurance has done its job and done it well. On the other hand, if customers find much to complain about, quality assurance has lost touch with their needs and desires. And the latter is always the case when specifications form the basis of product acceptance to the exclusion of customer satisfaction.

5. *Too much devotion to nit-picking; not enough attention to solving major quality problems.* The Pareto principle, above all, should be most familiar to quality assurance. It tells us that 10 percent of the problems facing us account for 80 percent of the headaches and costs. Why, then, do so many people in quality assurance preoccupy themselves with the other 90 percent of the problems, which will solve only 20 percent of the headaches (assuming, of course, the problems are solvable and quality assurance is totally efficient in dealing with them, which is seldom the case)? I have applied the Pareto principle to the analysis of our examples in Table 1.

Unfortunately, too many quality practitioners think that if they solve the greatest number of problems, they will have made a significant contribution. As shown in Table 1, if they solve problems #4 through #10, only 10 percent of the problem cost is eliminated. If they solve only the

TABLE 1.

Cost analysis of problems using the Pareto principle.

Problem #	Percentage of Total Costs	Cumulative Percentage of Total Costs
1	60	60
2	20	80
3	10	90
4	3	93
5	2	95
6	2	97
7	1	98
8	.8	98.8
9	.7	99.5
10	.5	100

first three problems, however, 90 percent of the costs are disposed of.

The Pareto principle is an example of the type of thinking needed in much of quality assurance today. Putting it another way, priorities need to be established in any product quality improvement program. Failure to establish priorities results in just enough nit-picking to invalidate all the other good things quality assurance does.

Perhaps another major reason for nit-picking is the desire to achieve perfection. The urge to be "pure" is strong in the hearts of many quality people because of their technical orientation. They are not satisfied until every "T" is crossed and every "I" dotted. The urge for purist perfection, however, is not only unnecessary but may also be costly. And in almost every instance, it prevents the job from being completed.

6. *Too much concentration on manufacturing; too little attention to quality of design and service.* Quality assurance too often docilely accepts the status quo. As a result, it is isolated from other functions and assigned to manufacturing. The emphasis is placed on achieving quality during the manufacturing cycle, but the vital components of design and customer service are ignored. It is only reasonable to expect that a product quality function assigned to manufacturing will involve itself almost exclusively with manufacturing quality problems and focus primarily on manufacturing goals, to the exclusion of other, equally important aspects of product quality in other organizational functions. A product may be well manufactured, but if the design is faulty or the service sloppy, the goal of achieving customer satisfaction will falter.

Quality assurance has ignored (or failed to sell top management on) the need to become involved with such specific activities as service training, advertising, parts distribution, technical publications, warehousing, design reviews, and pilot plants. Without this inclusive involvement, desired quality levels can seldom be attained.

7. *Too much time in the office; not enough time on the firing line.* Many quality practitioners seem to be more comfortable when they are dealing with things rather than with people. They seem to closet themselves far from the crowds and devote their time to problems that can be solved without interference from people. There is an insular, womblike atmosphere to that kind of workday. Without people intruding with their constant demands for decisionmaking, most of it subjective, there is no need other than to face those clean and straightforward problems that can be resolved on a piece of paper or in the laboratory. Regrettably, the type of problems that can be unraveled that easily is not usually the type that exerts a major impact on product quality.

There is also the pernicious tendency of subordinates to tell their boss only what they want him to know, thereby isolating him even more from the realities.

A quality assurance manager who shies away from the factory floor, customers, design engineers, vendors, inspectors, servicemen, and other people key to quality is only damaging his chances of keeping abreast on what is really happening on the firing line. The stories he gets from operators on the line may not even faintly resemble those beautifully prepared graphs on prominent display in his office.

8. *Too much technical education for quality assurance technicians; too little practical education of operators, draftsmen, servicemen, and others responsible for getting quality.* Again, the unholy absorption with technical matters detracts quality assurance from the real job at hand—teaching quality techniques to people who design, build, install, and service the product. It is abundantly clear that the most knowledgeable and sophisticated quality practitioners can contribute just so much to improving quality levels. Quality assurance does not

design the product, build it, install it, or service it. Those tasks are accomplished by engineers, operators, salesmen, and servicemen. It stands to reason that poor quality will result if those people do not understand the significance of quality and are unaware of how to achieve it.

9. *Too heavy a focus on quality levels; not enough devotion to quality cost reduction.* I'm sure many of you are familiar with companies that have protected their quality levels in the field by bottling up the shipping departments' doors. Sure, their customer satisfaction is high and their warranty costs are low, but if quality assurance isn't doing the job in the factories, scrap, rework, and sorting costs are bound to be prohibitively high.

The job of quality assurance isn't done until quality costs have been reduced to accepted and budgeted levels. It does little good to please customers if costs are so high that you either have to lose money or pass the loss on to customers by raising prices. This is not an extreme case, either. I know of *many* companies that have been forced to raise prices to keep from suffering losses because of high quality costs. A lot of companies unfamiliar with electronics, for example, have experienced quality costs of up to 30 percent of sales when they switched their product lines from electromechanical to electronic drives and controls. When that happens—and it happens frequently—you can bet quality assurance was caught with its pants down when the switch was made.

Quality costs are still too high in more stable product situations. Even without the burden of new electronic products, a great many companies have quality costs running at 10 percent of sales. They may not even know it, either because they lack cost-of-quality reporting or because all quality costs are not tabulated. A professional quality team will not only assure itself of fully reported quality costs, it will also do whatever needs to be done to get those costs in line with sales at acceptable levels.

10. *Too much time spent complaining about poor attitudes toward quality; not enough focus on motivating people and convincing them of the value of quality.* I sometimes think that the worst fault of quality practitioners is their failure as salesmen. Whatever the job to be done, improvements must first be sold to top management and then to the people who design, build, install, and service the product. Unless those people are convinced of the merits of quality, it just won't be achieved. *Selling the concept is the very first step to be undertaken when installing an effective quality program. Without success at that beginning stage, no success can follow, regardless of how potent the arsenal of quality techniques to follow.*

When quality assurance does not possess the ability to sell itself, quality will wither and die. That's when quality practitioners start griping about the poor attitudes toward quality of others in the organization. When that telltale sign appears, it is a sure indictment of the quality assurance team and a measure of its impotence.

And it is all too common.

2. *Stale Leadership*

A quality assurance manager I once knew had had the opportunity to work for a dynamic director of quality assurance. This director had been hired to turn around the product quality effort. Using a multitude of productive techniques the director did, indeed, turn the direction of product quality around. Within a relatively short period of time quality costs were substantially reduced and the company's product quality reputation improved enormously.

The quality assurance manager was inordinately impressed by the achievements of his boss, the director. He studied closely and noted carefully all the steps the director had taken. After a three-year stewardship he changed companies to become a director of quality himself. He felt that he was ready to assume the responsibilities of the number one spot in product and service quality.

Without hesitation he began implementing those systems he had learned from his boss during his previous job. He reorganized quality functions in manufacturing, product engineering, and marketing. He installed the exact same systems his boss had used in exactly the same manner. He did nothing to tailor the systems to the new organization; instead he used the very same procedures and forms that had been used by his former employer.

Within a three-month period the results of his efforts proved to be a mixed bag; some of the new programs were moderately successful, but most were not. Everybody was puzzled: the top executive who had hired the quality assurance man, the executive recruiter who had placed him, and the new quality director's peers. His ideas had seemed to be appropriate and timely. Probably the most surprised person of all was the new quality director himself. He had seen all the programs he had installed work wonders at his former company, and he couldn't understand why they hadn't worked well in the new environment.

Those words are key: "the new environment." The quality director had not been astute enough to know that quality systems, like all other systems, must *always* be tailored to the operations they are servicing. Products are different, processes are different, and so are plant layouts, management philosophies, and operating procedures, as well as a host of other factors. It is most improbable that a quality system found in one company will be successful in another company without some modifications.

Even the same company, with similar plants operating in

proximity to one another, may need different systems to accommodate differences in peoples' attitudes alone. One plant, for example, may be unionized, while the adjacent plant isn't. Most probably the unionized plant will need a control system that is more extensive than that of the non-union plant (it could also be the other way around).

Another difference requiring a tailoring of the approach would be worker seniority. If the average seniority in one plant is 20 years, chances are workers' quality will be superior to that of workers in the sister plant, where the average seniority is three years. Experience does have its value. (Again, the reverse could be true; youthful exuberance does much to balance older workers' experience.) The point is, however, that quality systems can never be adapted whole hog. They must be "hand-fitted" in every single adaptation.

Stale leadership is the disease of facing today's opportunities with yesterday's solutions. It is the unthinking application of experience without due regard for changing conditions. Since little remains unchanged in today's environment, it is only to be expected that quality systems must be changed too. Even within the same environment, factors change with the passage of time. What was once acceptable is passé and ineffective today. New approaches must be devised.

A new company needs a functional quality organization geared to training people in quality and devising systems to support that effort. A more mature company, on the other hand, has a strong need for a line quality organization to carry on its day-to-day activities. Each need must be assessed in its own right.

Stale leadership has been a prime contributor to the quality problems we are experiencing today. To cancel its deleterious effects, quality leadership must demonstrate the ability to think problems through to workable solutions.

3. A Bag of Magic Dust

Many companies recognize when they need to change from inspection-oriented product acceptance systems to professionally planned quality programs. The recognition may come slowly, but it becomes an inexorable conclusion when business and customers are lost because of poor quality or when failure costs skyrocket. At that stage, top management may understand it is in trouble, but not know how to handle it or what kinds of changes it should institute.

In almost every case, the answer is to go outside the company and look for a quality professional who can turn quality around, restore the company's quality image, and reduce its quality costs.

Fine and dandy! That sounds like a good beginning step for companies just awakening to the fact that they have severe quality problems. The problems, however, intensify rather than abate once the new quality persons come on board. It is at that stage that many company managements sigh with relief, smile, and then forget about their quality problems. After all, they have hired quality professionals, haven't they? The new people will handle all the quality problems, won't they?

No, they won't.

Quality professionals can establish the systems, put in and monitor the controls, train and develop people to the new quality methods, change attitudes (the hardest job of all), *but they can't do the jobs of designing, manufacturing, and servicing the products.* Those are rightfully the jobs of engineering, manufacturing, and marketing, and the quality aspects of those jobs are their responsibility as well.

Quality is the responsibility of general management, not of the

*quality professionals. And unless that very basic and necessary
tenet is understood and practiced, quality will never happen.*

There just aren't any miracles in the area of quality. The
new quality professionals don't have bags of magic dust which
they can take out and sprinkle on the problems, making them
disappear miraculously.

From a broad, conceptual point of view, there are two
primary ingredients in the successful execution of a quality
program. First, do the right things to improve quality, and
second, get the right top management support and commitment.

When top management refuses to face up to its responsibilities to obtain quality, all the magicians in the world and
their bags of magic dust will come to naught. Top management must be involved up to its eyebrows.

4. *Too Many Statistics,* *Not Enough Sense*

I sometimes wish the science of statistics—as helpful as it
is—had never been developed. It has set the efforts of quality
assurance to professionalize itself back by 50 years; not because statistics is a bad thing—it's an excellent tool when used
properly—but because so many managers have relied exclusively on it to deliver results. As you have gathered from
what you have read so far, many quality practitioners experience an almost overwhelming compulsion to rely on what is
scientific and numerical without regard for commensense interpretation and exercise of good judgment. Probably more
than any other single factor, this exclusionary reliance on

technology has damaged both the reputation of quality assurance and its ability to do its job. And nowhere is that factor more evident than in the use of statistics.

Let's start with some concrete examples and then explain the consequences.

One major heavy equipment manufacturer in the Midwest decided to apply narrow-limit gauging to approve setups for grinding machines in its large machine shop. Narrow-limit gauging starts with established specifications and narrows the acceptance range to one that is tighter than specifications, which indicates control of the process.

Quality engineers established ranges for all 30 grinders. Operators were trained to use the gauging and charting techniques and all needed supplies were made available. Within three days after narrow-limit gauging had been instituted, almost every grinding operation in the department came to a screeching halt.

A hasty investigation by an anxious plant manager and an even more anxious quality engineer quickly revealed that set-up values to qualify grinding operations were falling outside of control limits, although all values recorded did meet specifications.

The plant manager stormed off the floor berating the quality engineer and flew into the quality assurance manager's office in a near rage. He told both men to remove the narrow-limit acceptance technique, and then described in very colorful language where they should put it next.

Both quality men withdrew the new technique but decided to investigate and uncover the reason for the failure of the narrow-limit gauging. It didn't take them too long to discover that the technique had been successful on the few relatively new grinders but had failed on the rest of the machines, which were much older, some grinders dating back 15 years. They quickly connected that fact with the ability of the newer machines to hold control limits while admitting the older machines weren't holding them because of wear of bearings, ways, and other machine components. The older machines were holding product specification limits almost all the time but were unable to produce any work with narrower tolerances, which the new technique demanded.

Needless to say, quality assurance badly damaged its reputation. The plant manager thought it consisted of a bunch of fools, and quality assurance's peer group thought the same. Can you imagine the plant manager's reaction when quality assurance next asks permission to install some new system or quality technique? If only they had thought out the possible consequences ahead of time and had made just a few experimental runs before installing the technique on every machine. They would quickly have discovered the problem and avoided all that humiliation and potential loss of quality assurance effectiveness.

Their complete reliance on the statistical part of narrow-limit gauging was the core reason for their failure. Narrow-limit gauging—like any statistical tool—is a good technique, and if used properly, with a judicious exercise of common sense and knowledge of the process and product, will produce the desired results.

In another instance a large automotive company decided to install Shewhart control charts * on all its assembly lines for all six of its plants to control fastener torque statistically. The technique was well thought out by qualified engineers and statisticians at corporate headquarters; an extremely easy-to-read instruction manual was provided; capable engineers were sent to each of the six plants to aid in the installation and early use of the control charts; key people at the assem-

---

* The Shewhart control chart is a statistical method used to assure that a process will be able to hold tolerances.

bly plants were provided comprehensive training in the use of control charts by qualified quality engineers; and top management gave unqualified support to the program.

The torque control program bombed.

Why did such a well-conceived, well-planned, and well-executed program go bust? Simply because *most people do not understand statistics.* They neither know how to use statistics nor grasp the fundamentals of probability from which all statistics are derived. It has been my experience, as well as that of many other quality professionals, that only a very few people really understand and can apply statistics. And regardless of the hours of schooling and study and application, most operators, foremen, and technicians will never absorb enough of the concepts to apply statistics successfully in business and industry.

Whether this is true because of a lack of interest or aptitude (I believe it's a combination of both, coupled with the fact that most people have not had adequate immersion in the scientific method) is irrelevant. What is striking, however, is the amount of confusion and misunderstanding arising from trying to use even the simplest statistical techniques.

I recall when the purchasing department of a sophisticated manufacturer of drugs and medical equipment created thousands of dollars of unnecessary quality costs because of a lack of understanding of AQLs (acceptable quality levels). They were under the impression that if a sampling plan for one of their vendors specified an AQL of 1.5 percent, the customer plant would accept all defective goods as long as the 1.5 percent level was not exceeded. To make matters worse, the quality supervisor in charge of receiving inspection thought so too. For several months they accepted defective goods from batches that were lower than stated AQLs and were absorbing the costs of defects. By the time the quality assurance manager discovered what was happening, the company had lost about $30,000.

As you can see, even some quality practitioners have difficulty with statistics. The application of Military Standard 105D (an industry standard for attribute sampling), for example, is so badly mangled that it is a wonder it provides any protection at all. Quality assurance constantly misuses the plan, neither increasing nor decreasing sample sizes as designated by the plan to reflect incoming quality. It is also used in the wrong situations. Military Standard 105D was intended for use where the flow of work from a process is continuous. Using 105D to check but occasional batches of work often results in erroneous acceptance or rejection.

There are some very good qualitysense principles to guide the application of statistics:

1. *Never use statistics when you don't have to.* If the process or operation can be controlled without resorting to statistics, why complicate it? Provided quality level protection is maintained and costs are in line, there is absolutely no sense in using more complex methods. Stay away from them. Remember statistics is hard for most people to understand.

2. *When statistics must be used always use the simplest statistical technique available.* If you have a choice, always opt for the simplest technique. It will be easier to understand. Because of its relative simplicity it will be more fully accepted by people who must work with it. This principle includes using specification limits for control charts rather than control limits, and posting individual readings on the charts instead of averages (as must be done in bar X & R charts). Most people understand the relationship of individual values to specification limits, but go fuzzy when the relationship of averages to control limits is mentioned.

3. *Apply statistics only in selected operations, never across the*

board. The fewer the number of people you must deal with, the more successful your chances of a productive installation are. It is better to teach only a few people at one time how to use the technique than it is to teach 50. In the grinding operation example, assuming *all* the machines were new, it still may have proved exceedingly difficult, if not impossible, to install narrow-limit gauging on all the grinders simultaneously. Had quality management, however, selected a few key machines and installed the statistical method only on those machines, the narrow-limit gauging *might* have been successful.

4. *The use of statistics is expensive. Use it only when it can be justified.* "Justified" means that it either shows a cost savings or *proves* an improvement in the quality level. (Incidentally, any improvement in the quality level will almost always result in lower scrap, rework, sorting, or warranty costs. The use of statistics, then, should usually be justified in terms of dollar savings.)

Statistics, like any other management tool, costs money. The use of bar X & R charts, for example, involves such costs as training of operators, foremen, and quality technicians, calculation and tabulation time for maintenance of the control charts, and costs of reporting. These costs can be greater than you think. In other cases, the use of statistical sampling increases such elements as labor time, material costs (destructive testing), and training costs.

I recall a particular incident that should dramatize the point. A statistician working for the quality assurance department of a medical products manufacturer recommended the immediate implementation of statistically based sample sizes in the manufacturing process. He had been shocked to discover that *none* of the inspection stations in manufacturing had established statistical sampling plans in use. In every case, actual sample sizes were lower than those sample sizes specified by such stalwart plans as Military Standard 105D.

A study was then undertaken from which it was concluded that adaptation of the statistician's recommendations would more than *triple* inspection costs in manufacturing. A further look revealed that quality levels were high, and had been high for some years. That statistician was made to look like a fool.

Statistics is a very useful tool that should be assimilated by all quality professionals. Like any other tool, however, it has its limitations. Its usefulness must be evaluated carefully in every situation. Used properly, it can help get the job done. Used carelessly, it can actually reduce quality protection and damage the reputations of those who don't know how to handle it.

5. The Purists in Quality

Whether we like to admit it or not, quality assurance's reputation has been damaged because its ranks are riddled with purists. These types are found in uncommon numbers among technically oriented people, and quality assurance is certainly no exception.

Purists are compelled to interpret their experiences as either black or white tableaus; for them no gray area exists. When it comes to interpreting the acceptability of product to specifications, purists exhibit no flexibility at all—it's either good or it's not. To them, there is no middle ground. Their effect on the organization is deleterious. Since very few human endeavors achieve perfection, most organized activities—and products—contain some faults. The purist is incapable of interpreting the degree of fault. If it's wrong, he consigns it to the junk pile. His tendency, therefore, is to reject a product that may be acceptable—and that costs his company a bundle of dollars.

Purists are born procrastinators. Because so many decisions must be made on rejected products that fall somewhere between the extremes, they find themselves confused when forced to make those decisions, and they delay needed dispositions as long as possible. Eventually, they do make decisions—but they often make the wrong ones.

Most technical people work in an environment in which quantitative rules govern. The scientist knows that chemical formulations have exact quantitative compositions and the product engineer works with precisely specified tolerances, for example. These people, nurtured in a black-and-white world, many times have trouble dealing with less precise situations.

Yet the world of decisionmaking in a production and customer service environment is almost invariably based on data that are incomplete, if not downright vague. The quality practitioner is required to ply his trade in this milieu. Quite obviously, he must be the type who can react promptly to quickly developing quality problems. Time and production wait for no man. This environment demands flexible people, fast response time, and the application of good judgment.

The purist cannot cope with the demands of production supervisors and sales and service managers. He is totally out of place. He is slow, stodgy, and inflexible. He invariably becomes a bottleneck when he is involved in the decision-making process affecting the movement of goods and services in the product cycle. Whether on the factory floor or in a customer's showroom, he is constitutionally unable to keep pace.

Purists can sometimes be converted to action-type individuals if they are still young and their work habits have not yet been fully molded. It takes a lot of direction and patience, but it can be done. If, however, the purists have been operating as such for a number of years, the probability of conversion lessens appreciably. In those cases, the only alternative, unfortunately, is to remove them from their line positions and place them in staff jobs, where they will be more comfortable dealing with black-and-white situations.

But remove them you must! Don't delude yourself that they do the quality effort and organization no harm. They are largely responsible for the poor reputation quality assurance has. To support them in line positions is tantamount to forgetting about the type of image you are attempting to build in the quality organization. Your failure to face this unpleasant issue squarely tells the rest of the company that you don't mean business, and that you are unwilling to face the hard realities of doing what you have to do to get the job done.

6. The Costly Urge for Perfection

Most of the tool- and die-makers I have known are perfectionists; so are many research chemists, design engineers, scientists, mathematicians, and members of the entire spectrum of other specialties. These people are craftsmen who, in the truest sense of the word, have a great deal of pride in the work they turn out.

And, often, that's precisely the problem. Many toolmakers, for example, feel compelled to mirror-finish a stamping die when *no* finish at all is specified on the product drawing; many design engineers specify tolerances in tens of thousands when thousands alone would do; untold numbers of bench chemists insist on only the finest grade of chemicals when lesser grades will do the job, and do it at a lower cost without impairing quality.

These people mean well, but they are costing their companies untold millions of dollars because of their compulsion to do only the best work possible. They do not understand that it costs dollars—all of them wasted—to make products that greatly exceed company-specified quality levels. Their motivation is pure but their desire for perfectionism almost always results in excess cost.

These kinds of craftsmen are mostly technicians, but they can also be found in the ranks of management. Visualize, if you will, the quality foreman stubbornly refusing to approve manufactured parts until they have been inspected two or three times; or the accountant who hangs onto needed management reports until every single penny has been verified. This trait is partially attributable to insecurity; but most of it stems from a drive for perfection.

When an employee with the compulsive urge for perfection becomes a manager with responsibility for the work of others, his influence is multiplied. People working for him are driven to strive for the same level of perfection the boss exhibits and demands. Quality levels creep up and eventually exceed company specifications—and the performance of the entire department reflects the unrealistically high quality in wasted dollars.

A rough correlation can be established between occupational groups and the compulsion to achieve perfection. My own investigation and analysis indicate the following ranking, in descending order of magnitude, with the lowest level of compulsion at the bottom of the list:

Research scientist
Advanced design engineer
Mathematician
Skilled trades craftsman
Systems analyst
Bench chemist
Inspector
Accountant
Industrial engineer
Machine operator
Clerical worker

The list is only a rough guide. All of us have known machine operators, for example, who exhibit the craftsmen's urge. They could no sooner machine a substandard part than kick their wives and children. The concept is repugnant to them. But they are the exceptions. Generally, the higher the degree of technical specialization, the more compulsive the urge for perfection.

Managers confronted with the problem of excess zeal by its employees can return them to reality through the appropriate use of controls. The first step is to select work finished by their employees randomly and to have the work inspected and compared with product specifications. Work from any single employee consistently exceeding specifications will quickly become evident. Managers can then counsel the overachievers, explaining how their excess zeal creates lost dollars. Lost dollars can be equated with lower profitability, which, in turn, can be equated with fewer jobs. Even the most compulsive craftsman will understand the cost of perfection if it is properly explained to him.

If managers are astute in their dealings with employees, they will be able to stabilize quality at a level above specifications, but not so far above specifications as to generate waste.

The sensitive application of proper controls will curb the urge for perfection.

7. Horrible Happenings

There is no one in quality assurance who, at one time or another, hasn't heard these words: "How did this piece of junk get by inspection? This is a gross error. A blind man would have found it."

Words like those can be heard anywhere around the world where quality departments can be found. And at first blush many such errors *do* appear to be incomprehensible. I once worked for a major automotive company that had shipped a car with a clutch from one of its assembly plants. Not unusual, because cars are supposed to have clutches. Unfortunately, that particular car had an automatic transmission. To make matters worse, the car in question had been shipped to corporate headquarters in Detroit for evaluation, and the error was compounded when a vice-president of the company crashed the car into the side of the company garage when he tried to manipulate the clutch.

A subsequent investigation (and, as you can imagine, there was quite an investigation) revealed that the car had passed through some 12 inspection stations after the clutch was installed and before the car was ultimately accepted by quality assurance and released for shipment.

How did something so obvious escape detection? The answer to that, and to many thousands of horror stories similar to it, is more elusive than an explanation of the Bermuda Triangle. Somehow, these gross errors happen. Possibly it can be explained by the phenomenon we know as random occurrence (that which falls outside of probability limits), but I believe it is something more than that alone. It is too improbable that a clutch would have passed through 12 inspection stations without detection. It defies the law of probabilities.

I believe it was caused either by people not looking beyond their noses or by people who don't really care. Let's leave it to the behavioral psychologists to explain. The important point to remember is that it did happen, as incomprehensible as it may be, and similar incidents will happen again and again until the end of time. That appears to be the incontrovertible nature of man (and inspectors).

Horrible happenings are sometimes explainable, but not readily obvious. A medical products company producing surgical sutures packaged in plastic lighting reels once chastised its inspectors severely for accepting the wrong color reels. That had serious implications because different reel colors signified different suture materials. A mismatch could easily result in the wrong suture material being used by surgeons.

After the initial error was found, quality standards and inspection methods were reviewed and new safeguards introduced; operators, inspectors, supervisors, and technicians were reeducated; and new testing equipment was installed.

The next month the very same error occurred and, as you can imagine, all hell broke loose. This time a more intensive investigation was mounted, but nothing unusual was found. By all appearances, inspectors were making gross errors in discriminating colors. Nothing else was evident. As a result of the second error, all inspectors were given color examinations, but to everybody's amazement, all the inspectors passed the examination.

The error occurred for the third time the following week. Everybody panicked. This time, however, an astute quality engineer suspected a possible color change in the reels, and he processed a few pieces through each manufacturing operation. He found that reels were changing color during the sterilization process. What started out as a blue reel turned to a gray one, and it was going undetected because the group of inspectors checking the product *before* sterilization was different from the group checking the product *after* sterilization. Talk about lack of coordination.

So the next time your car rattles like crazy and your garage mechanic tears open the door-trim panel to reveal somebody's lunch bucket, or you crank your new lawnmower, only to find the cutting blade is missing, remember that horrible happenings are not confined to your plant alone. You've got a lot of company.

8. *Word Games That Destroy Our Ability to Communicate*

All vocational groups, such as quality assurance, have specialized vocabularies describing aspects of their work peculiar to them and to no other vocation. We refer to these vocabularies as "jargon" or "shop talk." For example, if doctors explain an appendectomy to plumbers using doctors' jargon, chances are the plumbers will be puzzled; the same bafflement will be felt by doctors when plumbers describe to them in shop talk how a clogged drain is repaired. That's shop talk, and in many ways it assists fellow tradesmen or professionals to communicate with one another in an intelligible manner. Outsiders overhearing one of those conversations probably would be confused, but since they are not directly involved in the trade, that is not important.*

Unfortunately there appears to be a pervasive urge for most work groups to use specialized terminology whether or not a need for it exists. The substitution of jargon for common, easy-to-understand words is becoming increasingly widespread. And nowhere does this urge appear to be stronger and more prevalent than in management organizations.

Progressing from the simple to the complex, the use of specialized—and unnecessary—management jargon has increased proportionately with the growth of business technology. Today many quality assurance people (among others) don't state simply, in easily understood, unequivocal terms, what needs to be said. Rather, they search about for sophisticated verbiage they think will make them look knowledgeable in the eyes of the management people they work with.

This preoccupation with jargon doesn't really enhance their images. On the contrary, it makes them appear pompous; more concerned with form than substance. An uninhibited exchange of jargon may be accepted joyfully among phonies, but when a "doer" comes in contact with this group, watch the fur fly. He is not interested in empty talk: he wants results.

Not only can the excessive use of jargon make its user appear ridiculous in the eyes of competent management people but, just as significantly, it can also ultimately affect the user's performance. There is a very real and harmful tendency to allow jargon to inhibit action. The user no longer

---

* Of course, when a plumber foists his specialized vocabulary onto an unsuspecting customer to make a repair job sound complicated and jack up the cost, that's fraud.

gets into the middle of things, flexes his muscles and mind, and gets a job done. Not this guy. Instead he implements, establishes, and orchestrates a highly structured and dovetailed program. The words appear so damned sophisticated that he substitutes them for action.

The end result: *nothing.* No longer does he concentrate on accomplishment. He becomes entirely contented with the words alone. He has displaced action with a pseudosophistication and effectively hampered his chances of doing a good job.

To give you some examples of what I mean let's unobtrusively listen in on some typical management meetings. (My God! No tapes, please.) On the left side of the page are the spoken words; on the right side a commonsense translation.

SOPHISTICATED MANAGEMENT JARGON	COMMONSENSE INTERPRETATION
"Have any of you gentlemen given serious consideration to the finalities as well as the possible contingencies that might arise should we jointly decide to embark on this undertaking?"	"Do any of you know what the hell you're getting into?"
"Yes, I must agree that you have evolved a possible feasible alternative to the problem, but for the sake of prudence, I would ask that you restudy existing options and analyze the potential consequences of your selection."	"The damn thing won't work, kid. Back to the drawing board."

SOPHISTICATED MANAGE-
MENT JARGON

"Before I hire this person I would appreciate knowing if he is compatible with and responsive to organizational imperatives."

COMMONSENSE
INTERPRETATION

"Does this guy know how to do what he's told?"

"Propagation of any form of noninterdependent activities within the established organizational structure can only result in abstruse results and negated personalities."

"If you guys don't stop fighting you're going to louse up the whole department."

"The efficacy of that approach should be subjected to the finest scrutiny available."

"Let's find out if it works."

"Gentlemen, it's time that you finalize alternatives, select the most feasible solution, and orchestrate an optimum implementation."

"Let's try out the best method."

"If only we could amalgamate our resources, I'm positive a mutually beneficial and optimized organization can be successfully exploited."

"Why don't we get together and try to do the job we're being paid to do?"

"I think it would be best for all concerned if we could analyze and define the parameters necessary to fit

"We need to write job descriptions."

SOPHISTICATED MANAGE-MENT JARGON	COMMONSENSE INTERPRETATION
our human inventory * within the structure of existing responsibilities."	
"It is my considered opinion that the task under study should be systematized and then accelerated in order that the organization maximize its utilization of assets."	"Do it, do it fast, and do it right."

Got the picture? Alright, then let's see if you've learned your lesson. If you've understood in the slightest the jargon you've just read, you should be able to interpret the following talk between two quality managers trying to outdo each other with their command of jargon.

"Well, Pete, we've finally got our Interdependent Human Engineering Indicator System on stream, and early indications are that each operating unit has absorbed and mastered all of the collective facets of the program. We've systematized the program, allowing for individual mobility at each of the operating units while concurrently providing for integrated input and withdrawal responses."

"Jack, I'm terribly glad to hear that. For some time I was quite concerned that transitional objectives of the system had been supplanted through use of subjective judgments and unthinking, automatic people responses. Frankly, that had me worried to death."

"No need to worry, Pete. That never constituted a major

---

* Isn't the phrase "human inventory" sickening? It makes you feel like pieces of stock sitting on shelves, waiting to be used.

problem. Right from the start we eliminated the inherent variabilities of human proclivities through rigid adherence to a programmed, digital procedure maximizing the utilization of the computer, thereby interdicting the predictable folderol of human response."

"That's great news. One final question, Jack. I hear that IHEIS [Interdependent Human Engineering Indicator System] will ultimately force the termination of variable human response through a homogeneous environmental process utilizing the latest cognitive techniques designed in sequential steps and employing instructional devices. If we ever get to that stage, just how secure will *our* jobs be?"

"Pete, I'm ashamed of you. When have we ever permitted the proliferation of potentially pernicious people problems to permeate our permutable and professional phase-in of perceptive propositions and programs? You should know better than that."

"Jack, you're so right. I ignored the pragmatic potential and prompt permeation of these program proposals, not to mention the penetrating protocol developed for peak promulgation and performance. Please accept my apologies."

Enough said?

9. *The Burning Love Affair: Quality and the Computer*

While working as a management consultant I was once assigned to find out why the quality system of a medium-sized consumer products company was failing to do its job. Field complaints were high, warranty costs were out of control, and in-plant quality-related costs had recently increased over 30 percent.

Yet when I began my investigation, I was told by top management that the quality department had every resource available to do the job and was using the most recent systems and computer programs available to assist it in its efforts.

After I had spent just a few days on the job, one fact became apparent. The quality department not only had the most recent systems and computer programs; it was inundated with them. All of those carefully (and expensively) designed programs were literally kicking out hundreds of pages of information daily. Every conceivable bit of data pertaining to the quality of the product was available to everybody every day.

And that, precisely, was one of the major problems.

There was so much information available on raw materials, components, manufacturing processes, the finished product, and field results that it was inordinately difficult to determine what was meaningful. Separating the significant from the insignificant became, in itself, a major problem. The information needed to control the business was lost in a morass of marginally useful and unusable data. Managers of every large department, along with the quality assurance manager, were at a loss as to which facts to analyze first. Consequently they were unable to confront the major problems.

As a management consultant, I had encountered this situation time and time again. Either too much or too little information was available to do the job. But it seldom stopped there. In too many instances the wrong information was presented, or the program was too technical to be understood by the people using it, or the information was programmed in such a way as to make it difficult to extract the necessary data. All in all, a veritable barrel of faults.

Those experiences, and many similar experiences by my associates, have made me realize what a poor job many of our systems and computer men are doing. For years these people have enjoyed privileges far beyond those enjoyed by other businessmen. For too long many of them have claimed immunity from the immutable laws of profit by cloaking their trade in the mystique of high technology. The program or the system itself has become the objective, rather than a means to an end. Cost and profit goals have often gone out the window in favor of technical expertise. And many business functions have suffered: production, sales, inventory, research, accounting, to name just a few.

Systems people, however, are only one side of the coin. How about the other side, the users of programs and computers? Why don't they knock down the mystique surrounding the computer room, and bring its managers to their knees? Surely, if they made their collective opinions heard, top management would do whatever was necessary to bring the systems function in line.

There are two reasons that seldom happens. One reason is obvious, the other more subtle.

The obvious reason is that most users barely understand systems. They are confused and bewildered by the seemingly complex jobs performed by computers and their supplicants, the systems people. It is human nature to avoid what you don't really understand, and that is exactly what is happening. The merchandising manager, for example, tells the systems man what his needs are, and then he backs away from direct involvement in the development of the program. He doesn't really understand what it takes to get the job done, and he is so blinded by the technical language used by the systems expert that he forsakes direct participation. The net result is one of the conditions mentioned earlier: wrongly derived information, or too little or too much of it.

There is also a more pervasive but subtle urge involved, particularly when technical people come in contact with the computer. Technical people—scientists, engineers, mathematicians—often feel vulnerable to criticism when they have failed to keep pace with the latest technological advances. They feel left out if somehow they have neglected to utilize the newest methodology. The more technical the work, the more urgent the need. That is why more scientists are attracted to the computer, for example, than market research technicians are. Nevertheless, both groups are culpable. Only the degree varies.

What, then, can be done to exorcise computer room witchcraft? How can a company assure itself that its systems and computers are geared properly to company objectives? And what is the optimum way to couple systems and costs to extract the best possible return on investment?

Let's examine what must be done to return systems and computers to a commonsense place within business:

1. Systems work, computers, programs, and all their attendant paraphernalia were created to provide *needed* information quickly and efficiently. A second major objective was to reduce clerical costs and processing time. A third, and final, objective was to use the feedback of information to control operations. There is no magic inherent in the achievement of any of these objectives—just the practical application of mathematical techniques by electronic and electromechanical equipment.

2. Many systems people have created an aura of mystery about their work. By doing so they have lost sight of the objective—increasing profits through providing a useful service. Technical expertise has become the goal at the expense of positive contribution. To get back on the track, systems people must be trained to gear their activities to profitability, like any other segment of the business.

3. A formalized procedure must be developed that will be capable of evaluating quantitatively, as well as qualitatively, the relative merits of each proposed computer system. Each step of the procedure should describe precisely how to determine profitability, cost, benefits, and any other significant criterion of the computer system during each stage of its growth: idea, proposal, feasibility analysis, simulation, and implementation. Only in this way can a poor system be squelched before it imposes a burden on the organization; and only in this way can the very good system be utilized fully and cohesively by all segments of the business.

4. Many companies apply a procedure similar to the one just described to justify and install computer systems. But some of these companies fail to examine them periodically after installation to assure their continuing profitable use in the business. It is to be expected that what serves best today may be obsolete tomorrow. Periodic and objective reexamination of existing systems will prevent the continued use (and possible expansion) of something no longer viable in today's environment.

5. Probably the most important improvement would be to have a hard-nosed nonsystems man or woman run the systems department. The foundation of this idea is the essence of practicality. A nonsystems department manager would frown upon any attempt to install an impractical and costly but beautiful "state of the art" system. He would have no sympathy for something that does not contribute to profitability. He should be a prime motivator, forcing the systems and computer experts, as well as well-meaning but unknowledgeable users, to focus only on systems that would contribute substantially to company goals.

The new manager could be drawn from many different areas; the only major prerequisites should be capability and a results orientation. Certainly every company has a pool of talent from which to draw this individual. A hard-nosed financial manager or a tough production administrator, for example, could undoubtedly do the necessary job.

The love affair between quality and the computer can be entirely eliminated if a company is intent on living up to its responsibilities. The return to practicality of the systems function can do much to enhance the performance of any business.

10. Quality Means Conformance

If you really want your quality program to get into hot water, ignore the need to conform to specifications and requirements. Nothing will sink the quality effort lower or faster.

Quality *means* conformance. Without it, there is no control over products shipped to customers. Failure to exercise control over conformance means excessive product variations in customers' hands; and that means excessive warranty costs and needless customer dissatisfaction.

As a consultant, I once analyzed the quality problems of the gearmaking operation for a large off-road vehicle manufacturer. I had been called in to find out why so many of its customers were experiencing gearing problems with vehicles in the field.

The most obvious fact was the 70 percent rejection rate experienced by the gear inspection laboratory. At first, I couldn't believe it; something was radically wrong. If the testing procedures were proper and accurate, then either the manufacturing process or the engineering specifications were almost totally inadequate.

A thorough analysis showed the gearmaking machinery to be fundamentally capable and the gear tests meaningful. That left the specifications.

Sure enough, a perusal of the gearing specifications showed tolerances so tight it was absolutely impractical to manufacture gears on any consistent basis to engineering requirements. An analysis of the gear rejection rate showed that the actual rejection rate resulting in either scrap or recutting (rework) was about 4 percent. The balance of the rejections were being accepted by engineering deviation, and that condition had been going on for many years.

In effect, quality assurance was accepting or rejecting gearing to one set of requirements but was making dispositions (accept versus scrap/rework) to another, informal, set of specifications.

What confusion! No wonder customers were having troubles with gears. The company just didn't know what quality level of gearing it was shipping.

When confronted with this piece of evidence product engineering bristled with resentment, and defended its pristine (and unrealistic) specifications by claiming that "we've got to keep these guys in production honest."

Of course, what it was *actually* doing was making those guys in production *dishonest* because there were no realistic and workable specifications for gear tolerances. The only recourse of the production people was to make gearing that didn't meet requirements and, because of the ridiculous requirements, there was a tendency on their part to ignore specifications altogether and to present any kind of intolerable product to quality assurance.

There can be no doubt that unworkable specifications cause excess costs and inconsistent quality levels. Without workable specifications control is faulty; it cannot be exercised properly over something that is wrong to begin with.

False requirements are also an impetus to dogfighting among functional groups in the company. If you can't rely on the specifications, subjective judgments are substituted to determine product acceptability. Since subjective judgments are personal and emotional by definition, everybody will have his own viewpoint. The variety of viewpoints is bound to stimulate clashes. The result—quality suffers.

Quality *is* conformance to specifications and requirements. If that condition is predominant people have a focal point of acceptability and a starting point for problem definition when things go wrong.

Chapter III

Establishing Successful Patterns for the Quality Assurance Program

Things do change. The only question is that since things are deteriorating so quickly, will society and man's habits change quickly enough?

—ISAAC ASIMOV

1. A *Quality* Assurance *Credo*

The credo for quality assurance is

1. Quality assurance is a profit-oriented, broad-based business activity.
2. Customer satisfaction is paramount.
3. Quality assurance must be organized for growth to succeed and flourish.
4. Quality assurance practices should be established for all operating arms of the business.
5. Product quality progress should be measured quantitatively.
6. Quality assurance must possess a technical capability equal to the technical demands of the business.
7. The company should have an active and aggressive regulatory control and products liability program, and this program should be managed by quality assurance.
8. Quality assurance must professionalize itself; nobody else is going to do it.

Whether you're a quality practitioner or an executive wondering how to improve product quality, it must have been discouraging to have read everything written in this book so far. It makes one uneasy to realize one's efforts and behavior have been dissected, scrutinized, and, in many cases, criticized.

My purpose, however, was not to ridicule or humiliate. I stand among you as an executive and a member of the quality profession. Whatever I said for you goes double for me. I've been there and back. I have only attempted to crystallize those negative concepts and actions that have not only produced ineffective efforts but have also caused many management people to hold quality practitioners and practices in disrepute.

Let's cross over to the sunny side of the street. Let's rethink our mission and learn what must be done to help us do a better job improving product and service quality. The balance of this book is devoted to that task. It explains those techniques and methods that have been used by successful quality professionals and that have been found in successful quality programs.

Let's first establish certain fundamental principles. We can call these principles a credo because, like a doctor's Hippocratic oath, they constitute the very essence of professionalism—in this case, quality assurance. The credo should be the bible of the general manager and quality professional and should form the nucleus of the company's quality effort.

1. *Quality assurance is a profit-oriented, broad-based business activity.* It should not be treated as a technical specialty. The ways top management and quality assurance view the tasks of improving product quality must be altered substantially. No longer can it be considered an inspection function; no longer can it be relegated to manufacturing or engineering and then promptly forgotten; no longer can it be separated from the marketplace and its customers; no longer can it devote its full attention to technical superiority.

Quality assurance must focus on profits, repeat sales, and costs. It must develop a business plan, just as other segments of the organization do. That business plan must particularize what tasks are necessary to achieve quality goals and quality levels established by the company. And those goals and levels presuppose the existence of a product quality policy, established by top management and supported by top management wholeheartedly. People in the company must be educated about the role of quality in achieving higher profits, lower costs, and repeat sales.

The person assigned to direct the quality effort must understand the relationship of product quality and profitability. To do so, that person must comprehend and appreciate all business functions of the company. Only the broad-based businessman will be able to manage any quality program effectively and achieve product and service quality goals the company needs to remain viable in today's demanding marketplace.

2. *Customer satisfaction is paramount.* In many companies, quality assurance has been isolated from the customer, and that's tantamount to suicide. The satisfaction of customers is the raison d'être of quality assurance; without firsthand exposure to the problems creating customer dissatisfaction, quality assurance is liable to miss problem trends in the field and lose its feel for the state of customer satisfaction.

It takes a third party (quality assurance) to act as middleman between the customer and research (product engineering). Quality assurance must determine what features of the product customers are dissatisfied with and then interpret them in terms the product engineer can understand. Quality assurance must then follow up to assure itself that the right design changes have been made to eliminate the problems and guarantee customer satisfaction.

Needless to say, if quality assurance is not actively engaged in keeping its fingers on the customer's pulse, it will not be in a position to recommend design changes to eliminate problems. What's more, if it surrenders this role to marketing, the product will suffer for it. Although marketing is in an excellent position to observe and report customer complaints, it does not have the technical perspective necessary to interpret corrective actions to the product engineer. This is properly the job of quality assurance. If it is doing its job, it will understand both the field problem and the design problem, and it will be capable of melding them effectively for the betterment of the organization and the customer.

There is a tendency on the part of marketing to reduce its level of attention to customers once the warranty period has expired, most particularly if the opportunities for repeat sales are negligible. It is important, however, that customer satisfaction be gauged *after* the warranty or guaranty period expires, and from then on throughout the life of the product.

Many a quality system has an excellent method of keeping its fingers on the customer's pulse during the warranty period, but stops abruptly at that point. Unfortunately, the customer still wants the product to perform its intended function, and he or she is going to get awfully mad if some design fault, which doesn't show up until the warranty period expires, suddenly makes the product unusable.

Quality assurance, probably more than any other part of the organization, is in the best position to monitor these postwarranty problems just as it does in-warranty problems, and assure correction by product engineering of major design faults that contribute to customer displeasure. The level of postwarranty quality has a significant effect on the company's product quality reputation.

3. *Quality assurance must be organized for growth to succeed and flourish.* Good organization has seldom been one of the strong points of quality assurance. Most companies have quality assurance organizations that look something like Figure 1.

That organization, as well as many thousands of others like it across the United States, is typical of the quality effort that stresses day-to-day involvement with handling inspection functions and quality problems (putting out fires).

However, it is dealing with *today;* it does not plan for *to-*

FIGURE 1.
Typical quality assurance organization.

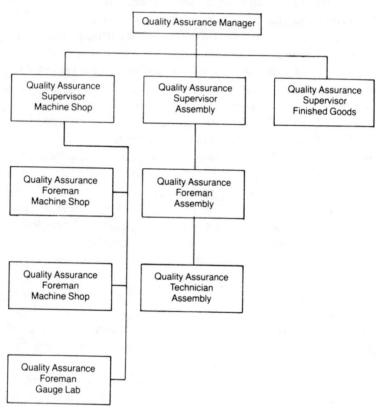

morrow. It doesn't have the capability for improvement or growth. As time passes, that type of organization becomes stagnant, simply because it has not equipped itself to handle future challenges.

A better form of organization is seen in Figure 2. The line quality organization remains essentially unchanged. It may have fewer supervisors if the "growth" side of the organization is effective.

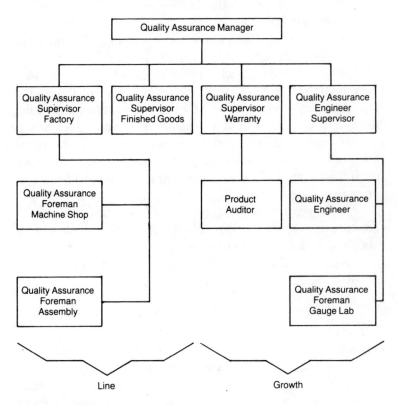

FIGURE 2.
A better form of quality assurance organization.

The "growth" side of the organization shows quality assurance's commitment to improving and strengthening the product quality effort. It contains a warranty supervisor. He or she is the person with a direct linkage to customers, salesmen, and servicemen. Through his eyes and ears customer quality problems are analyzed, interpreted, and fed to the proper component of the company for corrective action. The product auditor reporting to him assists in this work and audits the company's product to eliminate problems creating customer dissatisfaction from products ready for shipment. He is separated from the line organization because whatever he finds wrong in the product is not only a reflection of the job that manufacturing is doing, it is also a reflection of the job that the quality line organization is doing. His independence assures the integrity of his services.

Quality engineering, which works closely with the warranty section of quality assurance, is in charge of improving inspection methods and techniques and gauging, defining quality characteristics in new designs, assisting engineering in its qualification of new products, and a myriad of similar tasks, all aimed at improving product quality, reducing quality-associated costs, and preparing for the challenges of tomorrow.

4. *Quality assurance practices should be established for all operating arms of the business.* Most importantly, it should be established in the marketing and product engineering divisions where it has had but scant attention to date. Typical practices are listed as follows:

ACTIVITY	TYPICAL QUALITY ASSURANCE PRACTICES
Advertising	Review for technically correct and legally acceptable copy.
Service Training	Instruct servicemen to fully understand product functions and quality characteristics important to customers.
Technical Publications	Review for easily understood operating instructions and maintenance procedures.
Parts Distribution	Develop procedures to assure correct quality parts reaching customers.

ACTIVITY	TYPICAL QUALITY ASSURANCE PRACTICES
Warehousing	Develop procedures to assure proper storage, identification, and protection of products, as well as specified stock rotation.
Product Specifications	Develop procedures to review and assure whatever quality characteristics it takes to please customers before new products are designed.
Design Reviews	Develop procedures to review and assure that manufacturing reproducibility and quality characteristics are designed into the product prior to manufacturing introduction.
Prototype Reviews	Develop procedures to review and assure reliable product functions and product quality characteristics prior to sale to customers.

Quality assurance should establish these practices in marketing and research and continue to monitor them for results. The actual function is titled "Quality Engineering" on the organization chart.

Extending quality assurance practices to divisions beyond manufacturing broadens the outlook of the organization and causes a focusing on total product quality results. It forces management to evaluate the benefits versus the cost of product quality companywide and, by extension, the effect on sales and profits. It removes quality assurance from the boundaries of manufacturing and permits it to become a broad business function. Product quality is then defined in terms of overall company objectives and the philosophy of quality permeates the entire company.

5. *Product quality progress should be measured quantitatively.* Devising the product quality business plan mentioned before forces management to reflect and consider what it wants from quality efforts, what its costs should be, and, most importantly, where it wants its product quality level to be compared with that of competitors. Inevitably, this thought process results in clearly defined product quality goals, which, if assiduously pursued, enhance the prospects of the company through heightened customer satisfaction.

An important adjunct of the business plan should describe specific measurements to be made to gauge the achievement of product quality goals. For example, if one specific goal is to reduce warranty costs by 20 percent in the fiscal year, monthly progress should be charted. Should the plan falter, the company would be in a good position to shift direction to bring results back into line. It is apparent, then, that not only must the right measurements be made but they must also be timely, to correct deviations before they get out of hand.

The most basic measurement by which progress (or lack of it) is measured is cost of quality. The total cost of quality should be composed of the following basic elements:

Internal failures
  Scrap
  Rework
  Sorting of defective product
External failures
  Warranty and policy
  Postwarranty costs
Quality assurance budget costs

Most contemporary literature on cost of quality (COQ) would have you think otherwise. It would have you break down COQ into these broad categories: failure costs, appraisal (inspection) costs, and prevention costs. Actually, this breakdown is the same as the previous one, but restated differently. The conventional wisdom would have it that the greater the number of dollars expended on prevention costs the fewer the dollars that will be needed for both failure and appraisal costs.

That point is unarguable. The problem with using that cost breakdown, nevertheless, is the unfortunate tendency to make the whole thing a numbers game. Prevention costs, for example, would include the time a product engineer spends on building quality characteristics into the design. It is all too easy to begin compiling all these obscure—and hard-to-measure—costs at the start of a COQ program, then gradually shave them as the program moves forward. The effect would be a picture of a gradually declining COQ *although neither failure nor appraisal costs may have been reduced at all.*

The only hard, cold method of defining COQ takes note of failure costs and quality control budget costs. It is almost impossible to play games with these numbers. The movement of those costs constitutes the only objective and unquestioned measurement of COQ.

Quality costs should *always* be gathered and published by the accounting department. In this fashion the numbers published will be above reproach. When quality assurance publishes its own COQ data there will always be a nagging doubt about their validity.

For internal control of quality levels in the manufacturing operation there are two figures of significance: batch acceptance rates and process average defective. The former measurement is a direct reflection of the costs manufacturing incurs because of poor quality. If the drilling department of a machine shop, for example, processes 100 batches of work during a 24-hr period, and ten of those batches are rejected, their batch acceptance rate will be 90 percent (batches accepted/batches inspected × 100). Manufacturing will incur costs because it has to sort those ten defective batches and scrap or rework the culled defective pieces. Accordingly, manufacturing will always be most interested in those numbers, because they represent its cost of obtaining an acceptable product.

The process average defective, on the other hand, is a reflection of the ability of the process to hold to product specification limits and produce an acceptable product. This is the figure quality assurance must monitor closely. An increase in the index is an indication of changes in the process that will generate increased batch rejection rates. When that happens, quality costs increase. In that same drilling department, if inspectors had sampled 1,000 pieces and had found 55 defective pieces, the process average defective rate would have been 5.5 percent (sample defective/total pieces sampled × 100).

Suppose the drilling process average defective had the five-day history diagramed in Figure 3. Clearly, a negative trend would be evident. Should the trend continue it is obvious that higher quality costs would ensue. Using the process average defective, both quality assurance and manufacturing are in a good position to reverse the trend through timely corrective action.

6. *Quality assurance must possess a technical capability equal to the technical demands of the business.* Although quality assurance needs to be viewed as a broad-based profitmaking function, it must still possess the technical means necessary to conduct its business and achieve results. That translates into a fundamental understanding of product engineering and manufacturing engineering functions. If quality assurance is to

FIGURE 3.
Negative trend for drilling process average defective over five days.

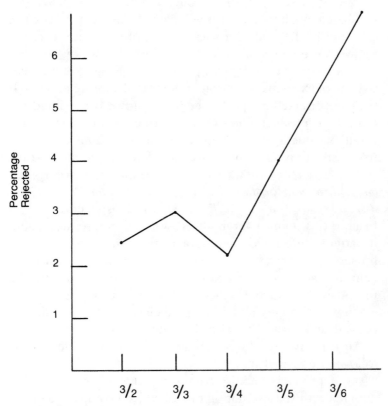

stimulate improvements in product and process design it must first know how to design a product, bring it to fruition, and establish the manufacturing process capable of sustaining the product economically.

Quality engineering is the segment of the quality organization assigned to handle that task. Quality engineers should have a thorough training in the engineering disciplines. It is probably best to staff that function with people from product and manufacturing engineering. They can then be trained in quality engineering methodology.

Capable quality engineers will have the ability to recognize and control the characteristics of the product that satisfy the performance needs of customers and will know how to identify the proper tooling, equipment, and gauging techniques to control excessive variation in the manufacturing process. If they are directed properly, they will know how to meld the efforts of product and manufacturing engineering into a profitable quality plan, emphasizing critical dimension control, inspection sampling plans, and effective product testing.

7. *The company should have an active and aggressive regulatory control and products liability program, and this program should be managed by quality assurance.* It isn't necessary to belabor this point. Everybody is aware of the products liability atmosphere enveloping American business today. Mere lip service to that function will no longer suffice. Any company not adequately prepared and organized to handle the formidable products liability laws is going to lose enormous amounts of money and will risk damaging its reputation in the industry as well as with the public.

An effective products liability program will contain the following essential ingredients:

(a) A products liability committee chaired by the quality director with representation of all involved company division heads, along with legal counsel and a representative of the company that handles insurance matters. This committee would guide the company's products liability program.

(b) An organizational component (normally quality assurance) containing one or more "experts" on safety and regulatory laws affecting the sale of the company's products. This is particularly important if the company is engaged in multinational business. Product safety laws vary enormously among countries, and failure to recognize the differences could result in lost markets and expensive field retrofits.

(c) A products safety committee with the responsibility of assuring that all new products meet industry codes and government regulations and are safe for intended use. This group, normally in product engineering, would be subordinate to the products liability committee and report to it for direction.

(d) A predetermined, organized approach for the handling of potential products liability lawsuits. This involves quick but thorough investigation of injuries and damage resulting from customer use of the company's products, and preparation for court cases.

(e) A comprehensive program in-house to gain compliance with statutory standards and to protect the company if products liability lawsuits arise. That would include, among other things, a plan for traceability of raw materials, proper labeling of products, adequate product warnings and instructions, and complete product quality records.

Assignment of the products liability program to quality assurance will guarantee top-level visibility companywide for this most important aspect of the business function. Conceivably it could spell the difference between profit and loss, as it has for several companies in the recent past.

8. *Quality assurance must professionalize itself; nobody else is going to do it.* I have saved the most important point of the credo for last. For too long now quality has taken a back seat to other company functions. As long as I can remember quality assurance has been viewed as a necessary evil and a place in the organization to absorb people who couldn't do a job in other segments of the business, from managers down to inspectors. How many times, for example, have you personally

known of cases where useless production workers have been made inspectors simply because there was no place for them in production? And how many production foremen and process engineers that you have known have been made inspection foremen because they were unable to hack it in their other jobs?

Can you imagine their negative attitudes and feelings? Nobody likes to be thought of as useless. How effective, then, can these people be on their new assignments? Similarly, how potent can a quality department be when it doesn't have the guts to stand up for what it knows is right? It is thoroughly demoralizing to be squashed time and time again by a production department in a rush to ship out a defective product.

What, then, is needed to motivate quality assurance to stand with its head held high? What are those intangible factors that can help quality assurance make itself felt as a positive influence on the organization? People in quality assurance, like people in other functions, can make positive contributions to company efforts *only* when they believe that what they are doing is worthwhile; in other words, when they believe in quality assurance as a profession.

Certain personal characteristics and beliefs can aid them:

1. *Quality assurance people must have courage and integrity.* They must *demand* immediate corrective action each time a basic principle of quality is violated. If a product that is ready for shipment has known defects, for example, they must stand up to production and prevent that product from being shipped or, at the least, make damn good and sure that top management is fully aware its production people are shipping garbage. If design engineers want to mark up prints to handle exceptions, quality assurance must prevent them from doing it. It must insist on changes to the drawings. If purchasing

pressures quality assurance to accept defective products from vendors, it must not buckle under.

In like fashion, quality assurance must at all times preserve its integrity. The entire company must have faith in its decisions. Its reports must go unquestioned or, if challenged, must be above reproach. It must possess the integrity and fortitude to communicate bad results whenever they occur, without ducking that highly unpleasant task.

2. *Quality assurance must stress defective prevention as opposed to after-the-fact inspection.* It is all too easy to become a finger pointer, a policeman. Anybody can do that. And it gripes the hell out of people to watch the efforts of their hard work negated by a quality supervisor who is not contributing his time to getting the work out. *Every person in quality assurance must work at corrective action.* Anybody who doesn't will never be considered part of the team. Quality assurance doesn't have the responsibility to correct problems itself. That is the job of product engineering, manufacturing, and marketing. But it does have the responsibility to help those people stand up in their jobs and *make things happen.*

3. *Quality assurance must stay in touch with the firing line.* That means getting out on the production floor, visiting customers, reviewing product problems with engineering, talking to vendors. Too many people visualize quality people as moles, ever anxious to get back into their holes, away from the battlefield. Constant visits to the firing line assure people that quality assurance is vitally interested in their problems.

4. *Quality assurance people must motivate others, not gripe and nit-pick.* The true sign of a professional is his ability to convince others that his course of action will produce results. That will not happen if quality people insist on nit-picking on minor product quality deviations to the exclusion of committing themselves to the resolution of major problems and the

making of meaningful decisions. It is also a mistake to gripe constantly about conditions and people's attitudes. That corrects nothing. The professional, rather, will motivate others to correct poor conditions. He will motivate others until negative attitudes are changed to positive attitudes. Then, and only then, will things begin to happen.

2. To Whom Should Quality Assurance Report?

The great debate still rages on. To whom should quality assurance report? Should it be to the product engineering vice-president? Perhaps the manufacturing vice-president? How about the plant manager?

Several organizational relationships have been suggested over the years and, depending on which book you read, quality assurance can report to almost any function of the business, as advocated by different practitioners. Let's examine the more commonly advocated structures and see how well they actually work.

Manufacturing

In many present-day organizations, quality assurance reports to manufacturing. The person reported to can be a vice-president, works manager, or plant manager, depending on the size of the company, the product line, and other significant considerations. The important point to focus on is the efficacy of quality as an integral segment of the manufacturing organization.

It strikes me that in most companies this reporting relationship has two basic disadvantages. First, the obvious one. When it gets down to the crunch, will the manufacturing boss sacrifice quality to make shipments? This is almost a trite observation now, but nevertheless we know he will. This opinion is shared by an overwhelming number of people, both in and out of quality assurance.

The question can't be overlooked, because both you and I know manufacturing has sacrificed quality so many times in the past, and will continue to do so today, probably as much as before.

The second disadvantage is less obvious, but much more important, than the first. Most of us realize the attainment of a high-quality product can't be achieved through manufacturing practices alone, no matter how outstanding the effort. It takes good design, good customer service, and a multitude of other factors to make what we now call total quality assurance. For example, manufacturing can do only so much to compensate for a poorly designed product. After that point is reached the product will still fail in customers' hands, regardless of how excellent manufacturing practices are.

Therefore, to be successful in obtaining a level of product quality that will keep customers satisfied, quality control must get deeply involved with other aspects of the business. But to do so first demands its organizational independence. If a quality engineer who is a member of the manufacturing organization attempts to impose product quality procedures within product engineering or marketing, he is most likely to get his hands slapped. Members of the product engineering and marketing organizations will resent his interference because he is a "manufacturing man." If that same quality engineer reported to the general manager, he would have a better chance of being accepted, or, at least, of having less resentment directed toward him by the people in product engineering and marketing.

Product Engineering

The comments made about manufacturing also apply here. To be successful in achieving high product quality, a total quality assurance approach is needed. The quality assurance professional working as a member of product engineering will encounter the same resistance in manufacturing and marketing that the quality engineer from manufacturing found in product engineering. The feeling of encroachment appears to run deep in all organizations.

Let's continue to be candid and admit the temptation of the quality professional working in product engineering to buckle under to the pressure of accepting new products when they are not quite ready for release. That happens more often than we like to admit.

Marketing

Again, the same comments made for manufacturing and for product engineering apply, but with one supplemental—and critical—disadvantage.

The marketing organization will almost universally ask for "perfect" product quality. It is normally the one segment of the company that fails to recognize that perfection is a goal rather than a practicality in sustained production or service operations. This attitude generally exists because the marketing man believes that if he doesn't require perfection everyone else in other parts of the company will do less than his or her best. He is also occasionally naive enough to accept his own pronouncements as gospel. In other words, he sometimes believes that perfection of product can be sustained indefinitely. Too many marketing people just don't understand the realities of production.

The quality practitioner working for the marketing vice-president often finds himself in the frustrating position of having to explain to his boss why the factory only achieved 99 percent quality performance last month. Regardless of his protestations that 99 percent is a remarkable performance, the marketing vice-president will not be satisfied. And, God forbid, should that performance be *really* shoddy, the quality manager could find himself in serious trouble.

With all due respect to our good friends and associates in marketing, it seems to me that having quality assurance as a part of their organization is a poor practice indeed. The time needed by quality assurance practitioners to devote to worthwhile projects will be dithered away while they find themselves in the vulnerable position of having to explain variances from perfection. Perfection is a goal, but to many marketing men, uninitiated in and unfamiliar with manufacturing and product engineering functions, anything short of superexcellence is incomprehensible.

Finally, there are some who are of the opinion that quality assurance can work effectively in any organization of the company. They feel that a strong, effective manager can surmount any obstacles and achieve product quality goals through singular concentration and dedication. You will often hear them utter words to the effect that a quality manager with a lot of guts and savvy can accomplish miracles.

It's just as hard to denounce that approach as it is to condemn God, country, and motherhood. The proponent of the "gutsy" approach is, in most probability, a gutsy guy himself who has overcome all manner of obstacles to accomplish his objectives. And he feels the quality manager can do the same thing. I'm sure most of us have met management people of that caliber sometime during our careers, and have admired their courage and determination.

Yet it's more than a matter of courage and determination.

To be successful it is also necessary to be smart and resourceful. And if working for manufacturing, product engineering, or marketing isn't smart or resourceful, then all the guts in the world won't compensate for the basic deficiency of improper organization.

Fortitude is a great quality. If, in this case, we can combine

FIGURE 4.
Relationship of quality assurance to other company functions.

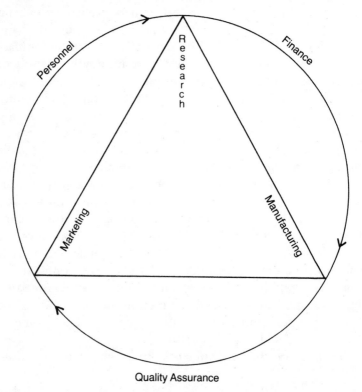

it with the right organization our effectiveness will increase geometrically. Why settle for half a loaf?

There is a growing concern today that quality, to be effective, must be on an equal footing with other segments of the business. This new school of thought advocates the separation of quality from manufacturing, marketing, and product engineering, the operating arms of the business. It recommends that quality be treated organizationally like the other support arms of the company, personnel and finance. Since quality assurance, like personnel and finance, should properly service manufacturing, marketing, and product engineering, the argument goes, why shouldn't it have the same organizational independence?

This relationship can best be illustrated by the diagram shown as Figure 4. The three points of the triangle represent the three basic operating divisions of most companies: marketing, manufacturing, and product engineering. The circle surrounding the triangle and tangent to its points shows the relationship of the three basic support functions that provide services to the operating divisions. Since quality assurance does—or should—service all three, it should report to the general manager or president of the company, along with finance and personnel. The organizational structure would then look something like the chart in Figure 5.

The recognition of quality as an independent—and important—arm of the business will automatically raise the sights of the company's product quality goals. It will also allow quality assurance to influence *all* segments of the company rather than its traditional concentration on manufacturing alone. The first industries to recognize and accept this concept have been aerospace, electronics, and other high-technology businesses. Given today's demanding consumer environment, the concept is slowly taking hold in other industries. The trend will probably not be reversed.

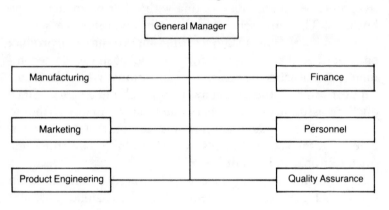

FIGURE 5.
Organizational structure with quality assurance reporting to general manager.

3. *Quality Policy, the Guiding Document*

Before any quality program of magnitude is undertaken, it is first necessary for top management to decide what level of quality it intends to deliver to the marketplace, as well as how—in broad terms—it expects to accomplish its goal. The result of such an effort is the quality policy, and it becomes the foundation upon which the quality program is built.

A well-thought-out, well-expressed quality policy will provide the added dimension of imbuing the company with a philosophy that extends to all its operations. It will outline objectives and strategies, and become the guiding document for quality efforts.

The most dynamic policies I have seen are not more than one or two pages long—but those pages let everybody in the company know the meaning of the importance of quality, what it intends to do, and how it intends to go about achieving those ends. The value of a short, general policy is that, although it establishes the general direction of the quality program, it does not limit the types of quality methods and procedures, provided they follow general policy.

Here's the statement of a major capital goods firm describing its quality policy. Notice its involvement with all major aspects of company affairs.

XYZ COMPANY GENERAL QUALITY POLICY

Purpose
To define the company's policy for quality.
Definition
Quality is the capability of a product to perform its intended function long enough to satisfy reasonable customer expectations, and to meet or exceed all implicit or explicit performance standards and safety and environmental requirements established for the product and support services by the company.
Policy
It is the policy of XYZ Company to deliver products whose quality results in performance, safety, and environmental factors recognized by our customers to be among the leaders in the industry.

Programs which support that policy are intended to reach every employee and all functional areas involving products shipped to customers. These programs include:

Product design and specifications
Purchased material, parts, and services
Manufacturing workmanship
Product and service support literature
Product sales and service

Strategies

—Our products will be designed to perform functionally and to be manufactured economically.

—Product engineering must recognize customer value in its designs as defined by the price the customer can afford to pay.

—Manufacture of the product will be in compliance with established engineering requirements.

—Manufacturing capability will be such that it can consistently turn out a quality product that meets customer expectations.

—Quality programs will be established for each area of the business necessary to assure customer satisfaction with our products and support services.

4. How to Improve Quality with an Action-Oriented Quality Plan

Once a quality policy has been adopted by the company, the time is ripe to think out carefully a plan of attack to improve the product, support quality, and reduce quality-associated costs. The resulting plan is embodied in a document called "The Quality Plan."

The quality plan describes quality goals, methods of accomplishing those goals, scheduled timetables, and people and departments responsible for goal completion.

TABLE 2.

XYZ Company quality assurance three-year improvement plan: key events.

Problem/Opportunity	Key Events	Completion by	Assigned to
Lack of direction for quality	Write quality policy and start quality board	3/79	President
Quality control organization ineffective	Reorganization	6/79	Quality assurance director
No control of manufactured quality	New quality systems in manufacturing		Quality engineering manager
	Purchased parts	8/79	and production
	Machine shop	12/79	manager
	Assembly	5/80	Manager
	Warehousing	9/80	
No quality procedures for field erection of machines	New quality systems in field sales and service	8/79	Field quality manager and service manager
No quality procedures for design and development	New quality systems for product engineering		Quality engineering manager
	Develop procedures	10/79	and product
	Implementation	12/81	engineering manager
Unorganized product liability effort	Revised product liability program		Quality assurance director
	Recommendations	6/79	
	Implementation	9/79	

Table 2 shows the quality plan for a capital goods manufacturer (the XYZ Company). The plan was greatly abbreviated for inclusion in this book, but it still contains the core tasks to be accomplished.

Please notice that most events shown in the plan specify not only quality assurance people, but also key functional managers, for completion of events. It is important to make those managers responsible for the completion of assigned events. That ensures their interest and participation.

Note also that this is a three-year plan. There is a reason for selecting that particular time span. Five years, a common period selected for making business plans, is too long for anything more than general plans; one year, on the other hand, is too short for adequate planning. I have found that three years is an optimal planning period, long enough to contain all the essential elements of the programs needed for quality improvement, yet short enough to contain specific actions for the entire period.

XYZ COMPANY QUALITY ASSURANCE
THREE-YEAR IMPROVEMENT PLAN

Basic Task

To improve product and support quality.

Objective

To install in manufacturing, engineering, and marketing an effective integrated quality system resulting in increased customer satisfaction and reduced costs of quality.

Goals

(A) To obtain industry leadership in quality by the end of this three-year program, as measured by an independent consulting survey of the industry's largest customers.

(B) Cost of quality measured as a percent of sales:

    1979 6.0%
    1980 5.0%
    1981 4.0%

Responsibility

Bob Jones, President
Peter Brown, Director, Quality Assurance

5. Evaluate the Total Quality System

Before the quality plan can be developed, it is necessary to evaluate the capability of the quality system to deliver a quality product with minimum quality-related costs. All aspects of the quality system must be analyzed, and from an evaluation of its particular strengths and weaknesses the quality practitioner will be able to rate the quality system's ability to meet company and customer expectations.

The evaluation is highly subjective. There is no easy way to assess many parts of the quality system. The extent of quality assurance involvement in product engineering, for example, does not lend itself to quantitative measure. Therefore, the evaluator must interpret his findings in light of his experience. That is very subjective. But there are no other alternatives, except to forget the evaluation.

The subjective nature of the evaluation procedure will not appeal to many quality practitioners. Their orientation has been technical and quantitative; they many times are not comfortable with issues that are not readily expressed in numbers. Nevertheless, an evaluation of the quality system is a necessary prerequisite for establishing a quality plan. The rest of this section is an evaluation format I have used often. It is appropriate for almost any type of product.

It must be emphasized that the evaluation survey described on pages 92–97 should be tailored to meet the needs of individual companies. A surface mining equipment manufacturer, for example, has a product erection cycle at its customers' mine sites that can last up to 18 months. For that manufacturer, an evaluation of the quality systems used during erection should be added to the evaluation survey.

QUALITY SYSTEM EVALUATION SURVEY

Plant _____   Auditor _____

Survey Date _____

I. Quality Assurance Administration

Organization

_____ What is the caliber of people in the organization?

_____ Are the manning levels adequate or excessive?

_____ What is the stature of quality assurance in the company?

_____ Is it respected?

_____ Is the organization geared to handle both day-to-day activities and quality improvement?

_____ Do the people in quality control know exactly what their jobs are?

Planning Capabilities

_____ Is quality assurance involved with all operating arms of the business (not just manufacturing)?

_____ Are planning methods satisfactory?

_____ Are there quality assurance manuals and a company quality policy?

_____ Are quality assurance supervisors given objectives?

Cost-of-Quality and Performance Reports

_____ Is the cost-of-quality program adequate?

_____ Is it used effectively for quality improvement?

_____ Do the performance reports contain the right information for corrective action? Do they identify trends? Are they kept to a minimum but meaningful amount of information?

_____ Are records maintained in a protected area?

_____ Do record retention periods meet federal and state laws?

II. Product Engineering Quality Systems

New Products

_____ Are critical, major, and minor quality characteristics identified on engineering drawings?

_____ Are potential quality problems identified early in the new-product development phase?

_____ Do design review procedures allow manufacturing to plan adequately for proper equipment, tooling, gauging, and so on?

_____ Are pilot plants or first production runs used to evaluate quality capability of product?

_____ Is a field (customer) evaluation made prior to release of first production?

_____ Are reliability techniques used? How effective are they?

_____ Is a quality engineering plan for inspection methods, gauging, and sampling plans made before production?

_____ Are new products qualified in engineering laboratory prior to release to production?

Engineering Systems

_____ Do you have an effective design change procedure?

_____ Is there a provision for disposition of materials when a change in design occurs?

_____ Are changes logged on engineering drawings?

III. Manufacturing Planning

Planning

_____ Is a quality assurance review made of major changes to the manufacturing process to assure proper tooling and gauging?

_____ Are machine and process capability studies made for new tools?

_____ Is quality taken into consideration in time standards to induce operators to recognize its importance?

_____ Are operators (not inspectors) given a sample plan for inspecting their own work, along with proper gauging?

_____ Are salvage procedures planned so scrap and rework are not mixed in with good parts?

_____ Does the materials system allow for traceability of defective work to individual operators and machines?

_____ Are operator instructions and methods adequate?

_____ Is production test equipment adequate?

IV. Vendor Control

Vendor Selection and Qualification

_____ Are pre-award surveys made to evaluate the vendor's capability to deliver a quality product?

_____ Is quality used along with price and delivery to select vendors?

_____ Is a vendor quality rating system used?

_____ Are quality requirements clearly communicated to vendors?

_____ Are drawing changes communicated to vendors?

_____ Are new parts from vendors qualified by quality assurance?

Receiving Inspection

_____ Are inspection and sampling instructions written and kept up-to-date?

_____ Are vendors notified of all details of rejections?

_____ Are records kept of vendor lots received, reasons for rejections, and dispositions?

_____ Are consistently poor vendors identified to purchasing?

_____ What action results?

_____ Are nonconforming parts handled by the materials review board?

_____ Are defective parts separated from acceptable parts?

_____ Is layout inspection capability adequate?

_____ Are parts not-to-print accepted only by written engineering deviation?

V. Manufacturing Quality Systems

Gauge Calibration

_____ Are master gauges traceable to the National Bureau of Standards?

_____ Are the frequencies of calibration adequate?

_____ Are the gauge calibration records adequate?

_____ Are gauges marked with last date of calibration?

_____ Are all new gauges calibrated before they are used in production?

Process Control

_____ Is the type of inspection control (process, tollgate, and so on) right for the need? Are written instructions effective?

_____ Does manufacturing have responsibility for correcting scrap and rework problems?

_____ Are inspection buy-off stamps used?

_____ Does manufacturing sort its own defective parts?

_____ Does the combination of operators and inspector sampling provide needed quality protection?

_____ Are quality cost reduction programs effective?

_____ Are the feedback and corrective action of quality problems fast and effective?

_____ Are the handling and processing of rejected parts timely? Are the rejected parts separated from accepted parts?

_____ Does production receive good support from support departments to resolve quality problems?

_____ Are operators provided with clear operating instructions, including inspection instructions?

Assembly Control

_____ Is the location of inspection stations timely? Are written instructions effective?

_____ Do sample plans provide quality protection?

_____ Are quality improvement efforts effective?

_____ Are assembly problems caused by prior manufacturing operations that are identified and resolved?

_____ Are quality standards the same between assembly and prior manufacturing operations?

_____ Do product audits reflect outgoing quality levels?

Packing and Shipping Control

_____ Is the packing adequate to prevent transit damage?

_____ Is the control of wrong parts and wrong number of parts adequate?

_____ Is parts packing checked against master parts list by packers?

———— Are shipping methods adequate to prevent transit damage?

———— Are parts and shipments well identified to prevent confusion?

VI. Marketing Quality Systems

Planning

———— Are contracts reviewed to assure the realistic attainment of specifications?

———— Are contracts reviewed in light of past quality problems for resolution in design stage?

———— Is advertising reviewed by product engineering and legal services to assure realistic statements of product features?

———— Is service literature reviewed for the same reasons as advertising as well as for clarity and ease of use by customers?

———— Is there enough buy-off control for trade show products?

Field (Customer) Acceptance

———— How effective are feedback of customer quality problems to product engineering and manufacturing and correction of the problems?

———— Is an analysis made of returned goods and field failures?

———— Is customer satisfaction measured (by audit) throughout warranty period *and* afterward?

———— Are customer complaint files adequate?

———— Are warranty charges made to appropriate parties?

———— Are surveys made of customer satisfaction and customer quality problems?

———— Is the training of field servicemen adequate?

———— Is parts service (replacement and breakdown) adequate to prevent excessive customer complaints?

VII. Training and Motivation

Systems

———— Is practical and applicable training given to operators, foremen, engineers, and other people who design, manufacture, sell, and service the product?

———— Is there adequate training for quality assurance management?

———— How are people motivated to do their jobs? What techniques and programs are used?

VIII. *Products Liability*

Products Liability Control

———— Is there an adequate product liability policy?

———— Is there a proper committee organization?

———— Is there support by top management?

———— Is there a legal review of all published materials?

———— Are codes, laws, and regulations met?

———— Is there an adequate investigation procedure?

———— Is systems control adequate?

The evaluation of any quality system must, by necessity, be long and detailed. It is only through painstaking attention to the details of all subsystems that improvements are made. Attention can then be focused on correcting the quality system's weaknesses to improve quality levels and quality costs.

6. *The Quality Board*

It is seldom adequate to publish a quality policy, write a three-year quality plan, and then stand back and let it roll. It just won't happen that automatically. Events of significance do not occur by themselves. They must be helped along. Even the most dynamic policies and plans must have life kicked into them, and that is the purpose of the Quality Board.

The Quality Board generally has as its members the general manager—chairman; the director, quality assurance—secretary; and the vice-presidents in charge of manufacturing, engineering, and marketing. Its basic function is to make certain the quality policies of the company are being discharged faithfully, and that key events described in the quality plan are being implemented successfully and in accordance with established timetables. The Quality Board also reviews and approves all major decisions involving quality improvements and sees to it that major quality problems are resolved by the responsible departments.

In short, it is the major impetus behind the successful application of a company's quality program. If you think it isn't necessary, try operating without it. Chances are that the quality plan will be implemented about twice as slowly or even not at all. The unfortunate point is that without the Quality Board, top-level management will not remain deeply enough involved with quality matters. It just has too many other commitments.

The Quality Board fosters top-level participation in key quality events. It provides the quality director guaranteed attention to those major quality problems affecting company performance. It helps promote the teamwork concept, and it allows each functional vice-president to have the opportunity to understand his peers' problems and opportunities. Most important of all, it keeps the quality plan moving and on track.

The Quality Board need not meet regularly, but it should meet when events need to be controlled and when major problems are encountered. At the inception of a new quality plan it will meet more often than when the plan and the quality effort are more mature.

The point to remember is that *it is the single most important quality committee in the entire company.* Used properly, it will contribute enormously to a successful quality program.

Chapter IV

Nuts and Bolts Methods for Achieving Quality Assurance

*If you don't know where you are going, you will proba-
bly end up somewhere else.*

—LAURENCE J. PETER

1. How to Control a Manufacturing Operation

After all the millions of words written on the subject in the past, when you get down to the core, there are only a few basic methods available to control the quality of a manufacturing operation. These are:

A. *Operator Inspection.* In this method, operators control the quality of the work they produce.

B. *First-Piece Inspection.* This inspection is properly used when the setup of the machine determines the quality of the parts. A production run of sheet metal stampings, for example, can have closely controlled quality if the first piece is inspected for size and edge characteristics. If both pass muster, the stamping press can be turned loose with the expectation that run quality will equal first-piece quality. An occasional check for edge quality (to spot tool wear) is the only additional inspection needed.

C. *Tollgate Inspection.* This inspection can be visualized by comparing it with the tollgate of a major thruway. Just as all cars must pass through the tollgates, all parts must pass through a tollgate inspection area before they are allowed to pass to the next production operation. Sample inspection normally accompanies the tollgate method.

D. *100 Percent Inspection.* This expensive inspection method subjects all parts to inspection.

E. *In-Process Patrol Inspection.* Inspectors rove from machine to machine, inspecting parts at random intervals.

F. *Automated Inspection.* In automated inspection, mechanical, electronic, or electromechanical controls cause parts to be subjected to automated testing equipment, and deviations to specified quality levels are corrected automatically by the process.

100

That's it! The six methods described above constitute all the basic inspection methods available. Although many manufacturing operations combine methods, there are no additional ways to inspect the product.

As you can well imagine, there are countless deviations from these inspection methods. Depending on the industry, company, extent of the quality problems, experience of the quality organization, and an entire host of other factors, different approaches are needed.

There is, however, a universal approach whose basics can be tailored and applied to almost any situation. I have developed this approach after 20 years in the business. It includes the recommendations of many of my contemporaries, most of them with considerable experience in quality assurance. I should warn you, however, that some practitioners will not agree with the approach I am about to describe, because in many respects it involves a major departure from the thinking of quality people over the past 20 years.

In essence, the first step is to turn over the full responsibility for quality to manufacturing. Most of the textbooks advocate that move, but few that I am aware of would go so far as to turn over to manufacturing all responsibility for inspection activities as well.

And that is the essential difference. Telling manufacturing it is responsible for quality is one thing; requiring it to step up to that responsibility is something else again. When it knows it will be required to inspect its own work, a discernible change of attitude occurs.

No longer can some manufacturing people say, "O.K., Mr. Inspector, you missed finding the problem, it's your fault." Now it's their baby, entirely, and it's absolutely amazing to see how fast they will absorb the job, and how they will do a much better job than if inspection were the responsibility of quality assurance.

In reality, manufacturing is given the job of first-piece and operator inspection. No inspectors are allowed to perform first-piece and patrol inspection. Those duties fall exclusively on the shoulders of operators, set-up men, and foremen.

Before those responsibilities are transferred, however, support must be given to operators in the form of:

Adequate gauging

Thorough inspection instructions, including gauging techniques, sample plans, and disposition procedures

Inspection training

Clear quality standards

Understanding of how quality affects the company

Operators will then be prepared to do the inspection job, and they will be aware of the significance of acceptable quality work.

What, then, is the role of quality assurance in a manufacturing operation controlled by manufacturing people?

Here the path diverges. It all depends on the level of quality the process and operators are able to sustain comfortably on a day-in, day-out basis. If the machine is old, for example, and the operators reluctant to give quality the full attention it deserves, quality assurance tollgates may be called for after each major machining center. If the process is under control and operators have a healthy attitude toward quality, fewer quality assurance tollgates will be required. It all depends on the situation encountered.

Needless to say, the role of quality assurance demands much investigation and is highly subjective. Let's walk through a few examples to sharpen your skills in this area. Assume three different machine shops, all with exactly the same machine tools and work flow, but each producing different quality levels. The quality assurance (inspection) stations would then be placed as diagramed in Figure 6.

FIGURE 6.
Placement of inspection stations according to quality levels pro-duced.

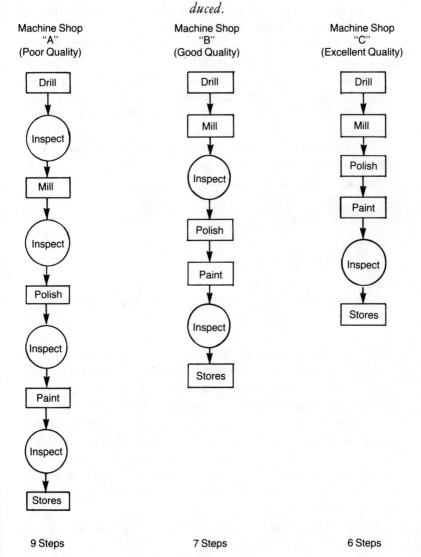

Machine Shop "A" (Poor Quality)

9 Steps

Machine Shop "B" (Good Quality)

7 Steps

Machine Shop "C" (Excellent Quality)

6 Steps

Obviously, the poorer the quality levels, the greater the need for additional intermediate tollgate inspection points. In a well-controlled machine shop a huge savings in inspection costs can be realized.

There are, of course, many other quality activities needed in manufacturing. These include such functions as gauge calibration, material review, and process control audits, to name just a few. But those techniques have been described many times in other books, and I have nothing further to say about them.

The decision of how many inspection stations to use, however, can go a long way to improving quality levels while reducing quality costs dramatically.

2. The Best Early Warning System

Early warning systems are designed to do just that—provide an indication of your product's outgoing quality level as well as highlight current quality problems. In most cases it is months, and sometimes even years, before products reach customers' hands. If companies rely mostly on warranties and complaints to assess customer satisfaction, the pipeline between the factory and the customer might be clogged with products that have a multitude of defects, undiscovered by the factory and inordinately costly in terms of repair costs and irritated customers.

Many firms conduct product audits to assess product quality levels, but few conduct them properly. They are seeking the best early warning system to suit their particular needs but, for one reason or another, they fail to do the right things.

A well-designed product audit is the best method yet devised to provide early warning of outgoing quality levels and problems. To be successful, however, it should contain the following elements:

1. Products must be selected randomly *after* they have been accepted by the line quality assurance organization and are ready for shipment to distributors or customers. The product audit is, after all, an indication of the effectiveness of the quality assurance organization as well as the manufacturing effort.

2. The product auditor must be independent of the line quality assurance organization that accepts the product. Ideally the product auditor should work directly for the general manager, but in practice that arrangement would be too cumbersome. Not enough direction would be provided by the general manager. He is too busy. There is nothing wrong with having the product auditor report directly to the top quality person in the organization. It is important, however, for him to be independent of the line quality assurance organization responsible for product buy-off and free from any pressure from it or from manufacturing people.

3. The quality characteristics being rated during the product audit must be the same characteristics that are important to the customer. *This is an extremely critical point that is most often missed by the majority of early warning systems.*

Most quality systems are geared to product specifications; acceptance is based on whether or not the product meets specifications. But the customer is totally indifferent to his supplier's internal specifications. What he wants is a product that functions properly, is aesthetically pleasing, and is safe to use.

While product specifications are generally defined in terms of customer needs, that is not always the case. As products mature they become subject to all sorts of compromises and modifications. Engineering changes, for example, are made to reduce costs. These changes may substitute materials that may not be acceptable to some customers; or part functions may be modified to accommodate manufacturing operations, and those changes might affect product function in customers' hands. All kinds of changes occur. Eventually, some product specifications become monsters on their own. They become self-perpetuating with no consideration of their intended purpose—that is, to consistently produce customer satisfaction.

Quality characteristics for product audits, therefore, should be established *jointly* by quality assurance *and* marketing. Salesmen and servicemen, in particular, will be most sensitive to customer wishes and customer needs. Many times the listing of quality characteristics important to customers will come as a surprise to quality assurance people, simply because they have been trained to think in terms of specifications and, as we have come to see, specifications drift over a period of time. The exercise of establishing meaningful quality characteristics will generate positive changes in product specifications.

4. The quality characteristics should be rated as to their importance. As Figure 7 shows, there are four classifications of defects ranging from "very serious" to "incidental." Each class is assigned a weight in points, with the most points assigned to the most serious classification of defects. During the product audit (see Figure 8) each characteristic is evaluated and actual points are assigned. Should the product auditor decide to assign partial points to a 50-point characteristic he can do so, provided that, in his judgment, some,

FIGURE 7.
Product audit classifications.

Points

100   *CLASS A—Very Serious*
  (a) Will surely cause an operating failure of the unit in service that cannot readily be corrected in the field.
  (b) Will surely cause intermittent operating trouble, difficult to locate in the field.
  (c) Will render unit totally unfit for service.
  (d) Is liable to cause personal injury or property damage under normal conditions of use.

50   *CLASS B—Serious*
  (a) Will probably cause an operating failure of the unit in service that cannot readily be corrected in the field.
  (b) Will surely cause an operating failure of the unit in service that can readily be corrected in the field.
  (c) Will surely cause trouble of a nature less serious than an operating failure, such as substandard performance.
  (d) Will surely involve increased maintenance or decreased life.
  (e) Will cause a major increase in installation effort by the customer or serviceman.
  (f) Has defects of appearance or finish that are extreme.

10   *CLASS C—Minor*
  (a) May cause an operating failure of the unit in service.
  (b) Is likely to cause trouble of a nature less serious than an operating failure, such as major degrees of substandard performance.
  (c) Is likely to involve increased maintenance or decreased life.
  (d) Will cause a minor increase in installation effort by the customer or serviceman.
  (e) Has major defects of appearance, finish, or workmanship.

1   *CLASS D—Incidental*
  (a) Will not affect operation, maintenance, or life of the unit in service (including minor deviations from engineering requirements).
  (b) Has minor defects of appearance, finish, or workmanship.

FIGURE 8.
Product audit.

CUSTOMER	CHARLTAN, INC.		RATING = $\dfrac{ACTUAL}{STANDARD}$ = 92.5%
TOTAL STANDARD POINTS	815		ORDER NUMBER WO45671-Z
TOTAL ACTUAL POINTS	754		AUDITOR A. Marasco

QUALITY CHARACTERISTICS	STD. POINTS	ACTUAL POINTS	REMARKS
Traverse	100	100	
Rest Plate	1	1	
Cone Holder	100	100	
Package Indicator	1	0	#1 spindle setting ½" off
Spindle Holder	10	10	
Cone to Traverse	10	10	
Package Brake	50	50	
Rotary Valve	50	50	
Package Valve	50	50	
Traverse Setting	10	10	
Traverse Shaft	100	100	
Control Shaft	50	50	
Reverse Roll (two screws)	50	50	
Traverse Brushes	10	10	
Package Valve (for nicks)	10	10	
Slubber Actuator	10	10	
Control Unit to Right	1	1	
Supply Rail Welded	100	50	cracks in welds
Supply Gears	10	10	
Supply Front Cam	1	1	
Trip Rods	10	10	
Supply Rear Cam	10	10	
Bobbin Ejector Cam	10	10	
Central Balloon Control Tubes	50	40	two tubes out of clips
Supply Reed Bail	10	10	
Separator Bail	1	1	
	815	754	

but not all, of the quality characteristics have been attained. See "central balloon control tubes," for example.

At the conclusion of the audit, standard points and actual points are totaled and divided to establish the rating. In the attached exhibit, 815 standard points are divided into 754 actual points; the answer is multiplied by 100 and a rating of 92.5 percent is obtained.

5. Defects found during the product audit must be traced aggressively and eliminated. This is the most important segment of the audit. While it is relatively easy to reinspect the finished product for defects found in the audit, it is much more difficult—but more necessary and more rewarding—to eliminate the cause of defects. The constant recurrence of the same defects signals higher rework or scrap costs, more defective products finding its way to customers, and, most importantly, a discouraged and dispirited management team that becomes increasingly frustrated watching the same defects recur.

A product audit constructed with the elements just described will be a powerful tool for management to use to upgrade quality levels and assess the effectiveness of the organization. A smart management team will take full advantage of this early warning system.

3. Incentive Systems versus Product Quality

An adversary relationship exists between the goals of incentives and the goals of quality. Let there be no doubt about it;

the greater the concentration on encouraging output the greater the tendency to allow product quality to slip. The relationship is not necessarily a direct one. If enough attention has been given to controlling the incentive process (tooling, materials, gauging, operator motivation, and so on), quality should not deteriorate as production increases.

The trouble begins, however, when a process is not controlled and reliance is placed on the operator to exercise due care and to inspect periodic samples of his own work. It is only reasonable to expect he will sacrifice any time he considers extraneous to making incentive pay. Inevitably that includes sacrificing the exercise of due care as well as reducing or eliminating entirely the samples he is required to inspect.

Assuming his standard includes time for inspection of samples, elimination of that step saves him considerable time, so in most cases he will eliminate it. Also, if the process is not controlled, even the very best efforts of the operator may not result in satisfactory product quality. The most conscientious operator effort may not be enough to compensate for poor material and inadequate tooling.

The key to good quality in incentive operations, therefore, lies in process capability. Unfortunately, that is easier said than done. It may not be economically practical, for example, to expend the money needed to bring a process under proper control. Process control can be, and normally is, achieved for critical operations, but a cost-benefit analysis for less critical operations may reveal the impracticality of exercising rigid control.

When that occurs, the only recourse is to establish operator identification of work performed and institute an inspection tollgate that will at least reduce the possibilities of defective work leaving the department. Since this is after the fact, it is somewhat less effective than process control, which is preventive and consequently a better system.

An alternative is to provide a system of rewards and punishments for product quality. In effect the inspector judges the work performed by the operator and, based on his decision, incentive pay may be added or taken away, depending on the quality of the operator's work. Withholding pay, however, is a negative inducement and doesn't always motivate the operator to produce better quality work. In many union contracts, for example, operators may be required to sort and rework on average earnings (actual incentive earnings for the department). The operator then receives incentive pay for reprocessing his own defective work. This is not exactly the best way to stimulate quality production.

On the other hand, why pay the operator a bonus for good quality when the very existence and meaning of his job demands good workmanship? If he is paid to do a job, it is reasonable to expect his conscientious efforts to produce acceptable work. But, as we have determined, the very nature of the incentive system may cause undue concentration on production to the detriment of product quality. In this case, the value of rewarding the operator for good quality work must be evaluated against the costs attributable to defective work. It has been my experience that a financial inducement for product quality counteracts the natural effects of the incentive system.

Incentive System for Inspection?

There are many recorded instances in which overeager manufacturing managers have imposed an incentive system on inspection. Inevitably, the result has been a reduction in product quality. I can think of no single case in which it improved product quality or even resulted in the maintenance of the status quo. There are substantial reasons for a negative outlook. When inspectors are included within the incentive system they are subject to the same pressures experienced by production operators. The more work they crank out the greater their rewards. It is only reasonable to assume they will opt for higher earnings. And they do.

Under the best of circumstances all inspectors, including the tougher ones, occasionally have the feeling their work is negative, that they are "ratting on their buddies." Certainly, if an incentive system is imposed on them, those feelings will be accentuated. There will also be the feeling that management can't be too serious about quality if they are giving preference to output over quality.

This is not to say inspectors are absolved from the responsibility for turning in a day's work. They most certainly have that responsibility. And it is our job, as managers, to assure that they are properly motivated and produce. But we must create an atmosphere that balances careful attention to detail with quantities of samples inspected. That is difficult enough to do without the added and artificial burden created by putting inspectors on incentive.

Should Inspectors Count Parts?

A closely related question is whether inspectors should count parts (normally a production or production control function). Many times inspectors will be asked to count parts, since inspection is generally the last operation in the order cycle in each department. Normally this request is accompanied by the information that no budgetary dollars will be added for the job.

Budgetary issues aside, I don't think it's a good idea. Inspection efforts will invariably be diluted, and the responsibility for lost and missing parts will become an inspection burden. Since inspectors do not produce, transport, or store parts, they cannot adequately control or subsequently analyze the variables causing lost parts. Furthermore, work-hours devoted to counting and checking for missing parts will expand and start to crowd out the basic inspection duties.

It seems to me eminently sensible to assign the responsibility for counting and tracing lost parts to those people whose prime mission is production and movement of parts. In this way authority and responsibility can be melded effectively and a better job can be done.

4. How to Control Vendor Quality–Simply

The literature describing control of vendor quality is voluminous. It also tends toward the complex. Esoteric rating plans, weighted averages, selection of price, delivery, and quality factors combined to form complicated mathematical formulas—all of these, and more, discourage the uninitiated. More importantly, they make an essentially straightforward task—improving supplier quality—hard to accomplish. They have the unhealthy tendency of focusing attention on the maintenance of paper systems to the exclusion of defect reduction.

I have found the best system to be the simplest one. Identify the problem vendors, bring them into your plant, discuss the problems, select the appropriate corrective actions, set a timetable for improvements, and follow up to measure future performance.

Notice that I didn't mention visiting suppliers' plants. That's not only costly and time consuming; it also doesn't have the impact of calling suppliers to your plant and giving them the opportunity to see the results of their defective product firsthand. There is also a psychological factor involved. When you visit suppliers' plants they will always show you what's right, not what went wrong. Needless to say, that doesn't accomplish anything. Identifying the factors causing the problem then subtly shifts to you, the customer. Their problems become your problems.

When you call them to your plant, on the other hand, you are, in essence, telling them they have a problem they must resolve in order to fulfill their contractual obligations. It soon becomes abundantly clear that the responsibility is theirs, not yours. Once that point is accepted, the actual resolution of the problem follows relatively quickly.

One company I worked for was experiencing exceptionally poor vendor product quality. Receiving inspection was rejecting 13 percent of all incoming lots. This intolerable situation was exacerbated by the fact that over 1,000 vendors supplied approximately 14,000 parts, and the inspection activity was not adequately identifying problem areas.

We organized a specific step-by-step attack that looked something like this:

1. A vendor rate of lot rejection was subjectively determined, beyond which that vendor would be assigned to our "problem" list. We selected 5 percent or higher as a poor quality rate, based on past history and our experience of what incoming quality should be. (Under more normal circumstances our target would have been lower, but in this case, we were dealing with an out-of-control situation.) Any vendor whose lots exceeded 5 percent rejection for the month would automatically be assigned to the list.

2. Lists were compiled showing inspected lots, rejected lots, rejection rates, and problem parts for each vendor over the 5 percent limit.

3. Rejections were categorized as follows:
   (a) Return to vendor
   (b) Scrap
   (c) Rework
   (d) Use as is (borderline rejections)

This step gave us the opportunity to determine the most serious and costly rejections. For example, if supplier *A* had a 20 percent rejection rate, but most of the rejections were "use as is," it would not be as serious a case as that against vendor *B*, who had a 10 percent rejection rate with all rejects being scrapped.

4. When all the lists had been compiled they were arranged in descending order of importance and discussed with purchasing. Further refinements were made at this stage, based on purchasing's knowledge of problems being corrected by vendors.

5. Using the final lists, vendors were notified of the problems again (they were notified of problems when the original rejections were made) but this time they were asked to come to our plant prepared to discuss how they were going to resolve these problems.

Over a period of three months all vendors on the "problem" list were consulted. It was interesting to note that in many cases the reasons for rejection were found to be different methods of gauging between the supplier and our receiving inspection. In most instances, the problem causes were more complex. However, it soon became apparent that the straightforward discussions were generating positive results. Rejection rates began to drop quickly and significantly.

In some cases we found it necessary to send a quality representative to suppliers' plants to analyze their process controls for improvements, but those cases were in the minority. When this step was found necessary it inevitably occurred with small-volume suppliers who couldn't afford the expense of quality assurance expertise. Within four months the rejection rate had been lowered from the original 13 percent to 6 percent.

One of the positive results of these sessions was that purchasing could no longer use the excuse of tolerating a poor supplier because "We're only a peanuts customer to them. If we give them any trouble they'll cut us off," or "They're the only supplier in the country. We can't afford to get them mad at us." Every supplier was put on the spot to solve his own problems, and it was obvious early in the program that each supplier was anxious to do a better job.

Elimination of these two prime excuses by purchasing gained impetus when the "only supplier in the country" for one of the problem parts failed to attend plant problem-solving sessions because his shop had burned down the day before. Concurrently, purchasing announced it had found another source. This surprising piece of news ended that issue once and for all.

5. The Importance of Traceability

If we were to single out the one most important segment of a successful quality improvement program, traceability would probably be selected. Traceability is the ability to identify the individual parts of any component, and that could mean people, tools, materials, dates, shifts, and any other particulars that pinpoint the origination of quality problems.

If, for example, a product fails in customer use, and it is possible to trace that failure to an individual part manufactured on a given day and shift, produced by an identifiable machine tool and operator, we could be well on our way to solving the problem.

One of the most difficult aspects of solving quality problems is identifying where and when the problem originated.

Without that information, the ability to solve problems decreases inordinately. If we don't know what caused the problem, it is only reasonable to expect that the problem will not be solved.

Traceability has other implications when it is related to operators, maintenance men, materials handlers, clerks, and other people responsible for doing a job (including management people). If people are aware defective work can be traced to them, they will be likely to take more care with their work.

That last statement was not intended to be cynical. If you examine it closely, you will understand that it was meant to help balance all aspects of people's jobs. Without some incentive to do quality work, the "production" aspect of any job is most liable to take precedence, and it doesn't make any difference if the job is that of a production operator, manager, clerk, or janitor. There is a natural—and expected—tendency for managements everywhere to get the most work done in the shortest possible time span. Without some countervailing force, quality is always the first to suffer; it is the easiest part of the job to let slip in the rush to fulfill commitments.

Traceability is that countervailing force. If John Brown stamps his name on the component he assembles, or if Mary White signs her name to the batch of paperwork she has just processed, chances are each will have enough pride (or fear) to allow quality to take its rightful place among other specified job duties.

Traceability in drug manufacture, as well as in other industries in which injury and death are a concomitant of poor quality, has reached the point where finished products are fully traceable to raw materials and to each stage of the manufacturing cycle. The trend is in that direction for other industries as well. Burgeoning safety legislation demands more attention to traceability in case product recalls should be needed, since traceability allows the identification and removal of "contaminated" parts or materials.

Until some of that legislation catches up with you, traceability can be made to work for you. It will help resolve quality problems and will instill a sense of pride in your workers.

To be fully effective, traceability should be established to the lowest common denominators:

1. Manufacturing
   Date and shift
   Machine
   Operator
   Material
2. Administrative
   Department
   Source document
   Clerk
3. Indirect Labor Functions
   Operator (maintenance, materials, and so on)
4. Product Engineering
   Engineering drawing
   Draftsman
   Checker
   Designer
5. Marketing
   Salesman
   Serviceman
   Contract
   Service literature editions

6. *Quality Techniques for Product Engineering That Really Work*

The application of quality assurance techniques to product engineering has not enjoyed wide acceptance. Most companies do not utilize this valuable device at all, and those that do mainly have limited programs. The acceptance quality assurance has enjoyed in manufacturing has not been shared with engineering.

There has been a great deal written on how to use quality techniques in product engineering, but most of it has bordered on the theoretical. Not too many companies today can boast of a workable and trenchant product engineering quality program.

Based on my experience, along with the experience of many quality professionals, there are certain universal principles. If applied properly, they can contribute to a dynamic product engineering quality program. As is the case elsewhere, it is the simple and basic approach that produces results and, conversely, it is the concentration on highly complex issues rather than on fundamentals that causes the program to fail.

Fundamentals of an effective product engineering quality program are:

• To plan what the proper role of quality is in product engineering, list all applicable steps in the new-product development process and, opposite each step, list what the quality involvement should be. Do *not* consult the textbooks.

Steer away from the theoretical. Combine good judgment and knowledge of your company's procedures with knowledge of the product. Ask yourself what must be done at each stage of the new-product development process to assure customer satisfaction with product quality and to minimize product quality costs in manufacturing. An abbreviated and simplified example of XYZ Company's new-product development quality procedure is shown in Figure 9.

FIGURE 9.

XYZ Company new product development quality procedure.

Steps in the New Product Development Procedure	*Tasks That Must Be Accomplished to Build In Quality*
1. Review new product idea with marketing, finance, and quality assurance.	Quality engineering to participate in discussion, reviewing quality problems of similar products and indicating what should be done to alleviate them in new product.
2. Conduct feasibility study of product costs and benefits.	Quality engineering to project all major quality-cost goals, along with specific plans for achieving them and relevant task costs.
3. Design new product and develop supporting assembly and detail drawings.	Quality management and quality engineering to review all drawings for inclusion of quality characteristics needed to assure customer satisfaction at low cost of quality.
4. Develop make–buy plan for in-house manufacture versus purchased parts.	Quality engineering to schedule all new parts for qualification (layout and/or testing).

• Identify quality characteristics in early design stages rather than after a product has been introduced in manufacturing. By including the identification of quality characteristics in engineering drawings and specifications, you are assured of a solid foundation from which to build tooling that will consider quality needs as well as a drawing that will provide acceptance guidelines for inspectors and operators.

• Rate quality characteristics identified on engineering drawings by their criticality. The standard categories of critical, major, and minor are usually adequate. Nothing more

Steps in the New Product Development Procedure	Tasks That Must Be Accomplished to Build In Quality
5. Develop prototype of new product.	Quality engineering and management to develop product-testing program; test prototype.
6. Review design with manufacturing to plan for right tooling and fixturing and selection of right equipment.	Quality engineering to approve tooling and fixturing to minimize quality costs in manufacturing and to develop gauging and inspection methods.
7. Conduct pilot plant run of new product.	Quality engineering to monitor results of each stage of the pilot plant to correct design and/or process and to develop inspection instructions.
8. Run field tests with new product.	Quality engineering to monitor field tests for feedback of quality problems.
9. Start production.	Quality management to monitor early production results for early correction of problems.

need be said here about the rating of quality characteristics. It has already been described many times before. The important point to remember is that ratings are used. All the published quality handbooks have definitions of critical, major, and minor quality characteristics with a cookbook formula describing their application.

• Test all new products under actual manufacturing conditions and debug before release to customers. As basic as that is, more companies than you can imagine don't truly respect its importance. More often than not the excuse of "no time available to test" is the prelude to an inundation of quality problems after the new product is placed in customers' hands. Another often-heard excuse is "it costs too much," yet how much more expensive is it than having the warranty costs start flowing and losing repeat sales?

There is a maxim that should be stamped indelibly in the minds of general managers and quality managers alike. It goes like this: "There is *always* time to test a new product." The corollary is: "It is *always* cheaper to test in-house than to have the product fall apart in the customers' hands."

It is hard for a product engineering or research manager to accept those maxims. He wants the product to be accepted by manufacturing, and any testing program will delay that goal. The marketing manager doesn't want to wait for testing results. He is impatient, wanting to deliver the product to hungry customers immediately. The manufacturing manager is being pushed for delivery. A testing program will normally delay delivery.

Who, then, is the party most interested in assuring completion of the testing program? The quality assurance manager, obviously. His life is easier whenever good products are delivered. But the real answer is the general manager. He must balance all functional requirements to arrive at the bottom line. Should he favor one or more organizational functions over others, he will be creating headaches for himself, because one aspect or another of his responsibilities will suffer. He must be big enough and smart enough to make provisions for testing in his new-product plans, and he must make it happen.

The manufacturing manager is another individual who suffers from inadequate product testing. If he is foolish enough to accept a new product within the manufacturing cycle without first having run a pilot plant *under actual manufacturing conditions,* he is going to suffer for it. I don't believe the product has ever been started that didn't display all types of unpredictable problems in manufacturing, despite the success of the new product in controlled product engineering tests. Too many factors are involved in the introduction of any new product, any of which can go wrong and seriously hamper planned results: tooling, material, manufacturing instructions, tolerance buildups, handling criteria, operator training—these and many, many more can have adverse effects if not properly controlled. And it is too difficult a task (and too expensive) to make such minute plans that every single aspect of the new-product introduction is fully and totally controlled and monitored.

• You should have written manufacturing instructions for each operation of the new product. They should describe equipment, tooling, gauging, method of operation, materials to be used, time sequences, inspection instructions (sample sizes, gauging, and recording methods), and other pertinent information.

Why should this most obvious statement be made? Simply because too many companies rely solely on the experience of their most senior managers and operators to manufacture the product. Ineluctably that leads to inconsistencies and higher than necessary costs. Unwritten manufacturing instructions are interpreted differently by different people and, as you would expect, varying costs and different quality levels are experienced.

The necessity of planning manufacturing instructions usually leads to optimum methods of manufacturing with its attendant high quality levels and low quality costs. That occurs simply because the more thought and attention devoted to the subject at hand—by trained professionals—the more impressive and the more consistent the results will be. Yet many companies pay but scant attention to the need for adequate manufacturing instructions.

Needless to state, there are many other techniques that pay dividends in the area of product engineering quality. This section was not meant to provide a complete text on all these techniques. Again, the standard quality textbooks do a very good job of describing such subjects as drawing change control, reliability, serviceability, and maintainability.

My purpose here was to describe fundamentals necessary to nurse a new product through the product engineering cycle, using those proven techniques to assure that quality has been built into the design rather than tacked on as an afterthought. The results are always pleasing.

7. Successful Marketing Quality Techniques

In all the published literature on quality assurance, only scant attention has been focused on those successful quality techniques that extend the quality system from in-house to the field. An endless amount of literature has described manufacturing quality systems; there has been some written material explaining product engineering quality systems; marketing quality systems have generally been ignored in published materials.

The productive use of quality techniques in the marketing area can be separated into (1) in-house applications and (2) field applications. The essential features of both are:

In-House Applications
    Warranty and policy claims
    Customer contracts and sales order documentation
    Sales and technical literature reviews
    Competitive evaluations
Field Applications
    Service training
    Response to customer problems.
    Machine erection (where applicable)
    Customer satisfaction surveys
    Postwarranty audits

A description of each of these features follows.

• *Warranty and Policy Claims.* Quality assurance should always have responsibility for the handling and processing of warranty claims; it should *never* be marketing. A major farm equipment manufacturer I once worked for transferred warranty and policy claims processing from marketing to quality assurance. The reason for the move was the suspicion of top management that marketing was "free and easy" with the warranty dollars in an effort to appease customers. Quality assurance staffed the warranty processing center with former service managers with years of experience. Their charter was to recognize legitimate claims but to turn down (or at least highlight) obviously false warranty claims.

These service managers were familiar with the product, knew the reputation of the dealers, and totally understood false claims when they came across their desks. Within the first year they were able to save the company some $2 million, and *they did it without alienating customers.* Some dealers, admittedly, were unhappy—but they were the dealers who were attempting to cheat the company. Customer service was unaffected, and dealers were forced to live by their contracts.

Warranty claims processed by the service managers were compiled by data processing into a computer run that detailed failures by failure type, age of machine at failure, dealer, state, dollar cost of repair, and other useful modes of categorization. The computer run was then given to quality engineers who identified repetitive, high-cost failures, established responsibilities for corrective action, and worked with the proper functions for problem correction. This organized approach to problem analysis yielded results. It soon became clear that quality problems experienced by customers were being resolved.

As an additional step, warranty charges were separated from policy charges. Warranty charges were defined as those legitimate expenses needed to correct customer complaints about the product *within the established warranty period.* Anything beyond the warranty period was charged to the policy account, a discretionary marketing amount, which marketing could award to customers if it felt it necessary to retain customer goodwill. The separation of warranty and policy allowed top management to trace the progress of warranty improvements that would have been impossible if policy charges—unrelated to the quality of the product—had contaminated warranty. It also gave top management the ability to monitor the extent of marketing policy "giveaways," which helped keep those charges at a minimum.

• *Customer Contracts and Sales Order Documentation.* A large plastics machinery firm in the East subjects all customer order contracts to quality engineering and product engineering review *before* contracts are signed. Product engineering passes on the feasibility of producing the plastics machinery ordered by the customer and quality engineering reviews contracts to assure that past customer quality problems do not find their way into the product. Quality engineers review each contract in detail, spot potential problem areas, and work with product engineering to "design out" the identified problems. They also let manufacturing engineering know what the problem areas are and ask that appropriate equipment, tooling, and gauging be used to minimize the problems.

Inspection methods are then established to screen out the residual effects not handled properly in the design or manufacturing process. Production supervisors are given "hot sheets" that identify the potential problem areas and the supervisors instruct their operators on proper manufacturing methods to minimize these problems. All these safeguards combine to assure top management that everything prudent has been done to keep recognized customer quality problems low.

In this same company, sales order documentation (customer contracts, correspondence with customers, inspection and test records, customer claims, and other written information pertaining to a specific order) are filed for quick reference in a vault. Documentation pertaining to any specific order can be located quickly. There are good reasons for doing this. First, in case of a lawsuit or claim, records are available for claim defense. Given today's demanding products liability environment, company records constitute a significant part of a company's legal protection. Since there are no federal statutes governing time limitations of company liability for products manufactured, each company is responsible, to some degree at least, for products it produced as long as 50 years ago. Therefore, pending a uniform products liability law, records must be maintained throughout the life of the product.

Quality assurance at the plastics machinery manufacturer audits the files to assure documentation is complete. When records are missing or when writing is illegible, the responsible departments are contacted for corrective action. Each culpable party is reminded that the product order filed constitutes a group of legal papers, and that the company must rely on that paperwork for claims defense.

• *Sales and Technical Literature Reviews.* Essentially it comes down to this: all promulgated literature should be reviewed prior to release to assure clarity of communications, technical accuracy, and legal propriety.

Company advertising should be reviewed by product engineering for technical accuracy and then submitted to the products liability committee or the legal department to assure that the advertising copy doesn't use any words such as "the best," "the fastest," or "the strongest" that are not truly representative of the product. Bombastic wording in advertisements has gotten more than one company into trouble in the courts when their products did not live up to the words that described their features.

Operations and maintenance manuals should be checked by product engineering for technical accuracy, just as advertising copy is. Then quality assurance should scrutinize each manual carefully for clarity, looking at the copy the way customers do, and asking itself if the instructions are understandable. All pictures should be checked for clarity and should meet the test of supporting the text where referenced. If a maintenance manual, for example, refers to a picture of an oil dipstick, the picture should clearly indicate the location and identity of that dipstick.

Warning signs, where appropriate, should be displayed on

machinery shown in pictures, and safe operating practices should be pictured. A stamping press, for example, should always be shown with safety guards in place, and prominent warning signs should be readable in the picture.

• *Competitive Evaluations.* Quality engineering, normally in conjunction with product engineering, can evaluate competitive products for design features, performance, reliability, and a host of other factors that indicate how the company product stacks up against the competition. This is a fairly well-used technique by most companies, and is well accepted as an important segment of a company's measure of its product's competitiveness.

Many such programs, however, fall short because they simply address the difference in product features. A very useful comparison can be made when quality characteristics are measured. This allows a company to compare its product quality with that of the competition and to make the needed adjustments in product design and manufacturing when appropriate. Although a fairly large investment may sometimes be required for laboratory testing equipment, most companies have found the investment worthwhile, since it allows them to monitor their position in the marketplace.

• *Service Training.* This area is a most rewarding one for the application of quality techniques. It has often been overlooked by quality professionals. Servicemen, however, greatly influence the *support* element of product quality. Regardless of how well a product is designed and manufactured, if it requires service and that service is shoddy and causes customer dissatisfaction, the quality reputation of a company will suffer.

Servicemen need to be trained to deliver a quality service in the same manner that factory operators and foremen need to be trained to manufacture a quality product. Servicemen must be trained in the right way to make repairs, to train customer mechanics, to teach customers how to use the product correctly, to maintain and repair the product, and a host of other factors.

Quality engineering, with the assistance of experienced servicemen, can establish a training program for company servicemen as well as for customer servicemen, showing them how to perform their jobs to keep customer satisfaction high.

Often good service can help a company's reputation in those cases where product failures are experienced by customers. Although customers will be unhappy with product failures, they can be appeased if the service is then fast and thorough. Conversely, customers will probably write off the company if its products *and* service are poor. So there is much to be said for service training.

• *Response to Customer Problems.* Without doubt, response to customer problems must be timely and must meet customer needs. The role of service has already been discussed. Another, equally important, area is the mechanism each company must have to resolve quality problems customers encounter with the product. After the service department has handled the immediate customer problem through replacement or repair of the product, how can a company assure itself that the problem won't repeat itself?

There are two recognized and proven techniques for corrective action of field quality problems. The first technique, used by the farm machinery company mentioned earlier, involves use of quality engineers to act as middlemen between the customer and product engineering or manufacturing. After a warranty claim had been processed, it was given to quality engineering to define the problem further, determine what caused the failure, assign functional responsibility, and follow up for corrective action.

Each quality engineer followed an assigned product line

and was made responsible for quality problems within his product area. He would assist product engineering in identifying what design changes were needed to eliminate the problem, or he would work with the appropriate manufacturing engineer to change the manufacturing process if the problem was attributable to poor manufacturing practices.

The philosophy behind this system is that quality assurance must keep its fingers on the customer's pulse, or it will not be in a position to recommend design and manufacturing changes to eliminate the problem. What's more, if it surrenders that role to marketing, the product will suffer for it. Marketing doesn't normally have the technical perspective necessary to interpret corrective actions to product engineering or manufacturing. Quality assurance does. It is in the best position to understand both the field problem and the most appropriate corrective action; and, consequently, to meld them effectively for the betterment of the company and the customer.

An alternative method for field quality correction was employed by the plastics machinery company described earlier. It formed a quality improvement task force to resolve field quality problems. Chaired by the product manager (there were three task forces, one for each major product line), representation on the task force included marketing, manufacturing, product engineering, and quality assurance. The product manager chaired the group because he had overall profit-and-loss responsibility for his product line, and therefore had the broadest overall view of the problem. He would not be inclined to favor any particular department, since he was responsible for total results. His focus was the most objective.

Quality assurance, incidentally, should seldom be put in the position of chairing quality improvement efforts, mostly because it then becomes just "another damn quality program." Nobody, other than quality assurance, feels any responsibility for making improvements, and that means nothing gets done. Almost always, a quality improvement effort should be chaired by that person most responsible for the outcome of events. In the typical company, that could be interpreted as shown here:

Aim	Spearhead
Company quality program	President
Reduction of customer quality problems	Product manager
Scrap and rework reduction	Production manager
Design quality improvements	Product engineering manager

• *Machine Erection.* Companies manufacturing capital goods machinery experience a common problem. Their machine erection cycle seldom has the same quality controls imposed on it that the manufacturing cycle does. Quality engineering projects, inspection methods and techniques, sampling plans, and the like mostly stop short at the factory door, hardly ever extending beyond to the field. Yet many machinery manufacturers have an erection cycle equal to or longer than the manufacturing cycle. Generally, the larger the capital goods produced, the more complex and lengthy the erection period. And, most significant of all, *invariably the machinery is erected on the customer's property, where he can personally witness every mistake company erectors make.* What more compelling need for effective quality assurance?

A machine tool manufacturer in the Midwest requalifies all its field erectors. Each erector is required to pass stringent written and oral tests at the company's training school annually and then is required (biannually) to assemble a machine in the company's factory under the supervision of a training supervisor and a quality engineer. That company's annual requalification even covers instructions on how to deal with customers.

That type of training was instituted because field erectors often complain to customers about the quality of machines leaving the factory. Without thinking, they psychologically ally themselves with the customer because they share the same frustrations when defective parts or the wrong parts become apparent at the erection site. That kind of grumbling turns off the customer, besides exposing the company's dirty linen in front of him. The training course at the home office shows field erectors the folly of that approach and teaches them how to deal with the problem.

During the erection cycle and again upon completion of the machine erection, field quality assurance auditors assess the quality of the erection through standardized checklists prepared by the manufacturer. These checklists contain rated quality characteristics similar to those in the product audit discussed in the section titled "The Best Early Warning System." In this fashion each machine erector has his quality performance evaluated, just as that of the operator in the factory is evaluated. The erection audit assures the machine tool company of consistent erection practices aimed at customer satisfaction.

• *Customer Satisfaction Surveys.* It is always beneficial, and sometimes necessary, for companies to conduct surveys regarding customer satisfaction. Too many times top management, deeply involved with the pressing logistics of running a business, loses sight of its customers' needs and desires. There is a tendency to delegate these kinds of problems to the sales manager. That road only leads to disaster. Control must be maintained over customer satisfaction just as it is maintained over factory inventories and quality. It is an ingredient that is just as necessary for the success of the company as maintaining low receivables and a substantial cash flow are.

Surveys are best handled by independent concerns that specialize in that kind of activity. It assures an objective, unbiased look at the state of customer satisfaction. The only major drawback is the independent auditor's lack of knowledge of the industry. He might, for example, ask customers the wrong questions, or address the right questions to the wrong people. Those kinds of errors can be minimized through preparatory discussions between the independent auditor and the right company official (only the general manager or quality assurance manager, *never* the marketing manager).

• *Postwarranty Audits.* There is a tendency on the part of marketing to reduce its level of attention to customers once the warranty period has expired, most particularly if the opportunities for repeat sales are negligible. It is important, however, that customer satisfaction be gauged after the warranty period expires, and from then on throughout the life of the product.

Many a quality system has an excellent method of keeping its fingers on the customer's pulse during the warranty period, but stops abruptly at that point. Unfortunately, the customer still wants the product to perform its intended function, and he's going to get awfully mad if some design fault, which doesn't show up until the warranty period expires, suddenly makes the product unusable.

Quality assurance, probably more than any other part of the organization, is in the best position to monitor these postwarranty problems, just as it monitors problems in products under warranty, and assure that product engineering corrects major design faults that exasperate customers. The level of postwarranty quality has a significant effect on the company's product quality reputation.

8. *Making Reports Meaningful and Productive*

I'm sure most people are aware of Parkinson's Law, which states that workloads will automatically expand to fill up the available time. An important corollary familiar to quality professionals is that reports promulgated by quality assurance are in direct proportion to the number of clerks working in the department. Amusing? Yes, but there is enough truth in that statement to sting even the best of us, at least a little bit.

There seems to be a pervasive urge for quality assurance to crank out voluminous reports whether or not they have a meaningful purpose. It's almost as if we feel more secure when we're flooding the operations with paperwork.

That urge is not only useless, it's also potentially dangerous. The more minutiae we generate to bury operating departments the harder it becomes to sort out and identify the significant from the trivial. Even worse, the people who use the information get discouraged and tend to chuck it all simply because they become too impatient to extract the control information they need to do their jobs.

It is therefore necessary to publish only that hard-core information needed to control performance and quality costs. My experience, along with that of other professionals, indicates the need for just three types of reports: performance reports, cost-of-quality reports, and special studies.

Performance Reports

Performance reports relate quality levels and reasons for rejections at different stages of the operations.

There is no need to emphasize the importance of immediate feedback about product quality rejections on the floor to responsible departments. As professionals we all understand the need to communicate quality problems for timely analysis and corrective action. This information, however, still needs to be collated and published in reports to assure detection of trends and adherence to goals.

Performance reports for a typical manufacturing operation should include quality levels for receiving inspection, manufacturing (machine shop, press room, paint ovens, and so on), assembly, product audit, shipping, and customer usage (warranty).

Product Audit. The product audit deserves special attention. It is a system designed to provide both management and operators with a view of outgoing product quality levels. In this system, randomly selected machines are evaluated after they have been accepted by the quality organization for shipment. The audits are conducted from a customer's viewpoint, with all quality characteristics having been rated previously as to their importance.

An important aspect of this program is that field sales or customer service people participate not only in establishing the ratings, but also in conducting the product audit with quality assurance periodically. This brings plant and field people together, with the focus on product quality making the product audit a positive stimulus for quality improvement. It should be emphasized that the product auditor should be divorced from the line quality organization to assure that his ratings not only reflect the effectiveness of manufacturing, but also the effectiveness of quality assurance.

The product audit system can be used for any product or any service, regardless of size or complexity. Although the system was originally established to evaluate large machines and machine tools, it has since been extended to include a variety of other products. (For a detailed discussion of this subject, see Section 2 in this chapter, "The Best Early Warning System.")

Manufacturing. Manufacturing reports should relate two basic figures. The first is the percentage of lots (batches) rejected. This is a measure of the quality job done by operating departments. It is significant to production people because it shows them how many lots will have to be sorted and repaired. Floor supervisors are responsive to those figures because a cost for poor quality can be attached to rejected lots. Since costs are the common denominator of production, everybody understands them and their significance.

The second figure is the process average defective. This number is obtained by dividing the number of pieces found defective by the number representing total samples inspected. For example, if we have inspected 1,000 samples during the week in a drilling operation and found 20 defectives, the process average defective is

$$\frac{\text{Number rejected}}{\text{Number inspected}} = \frac{20}{1,000} = .02 \text{ (or 2 percent)}.$$

For the quality practitioner, that number is at least as important as the percentage of lots rejected because it demonstrates the basic capability of the process (which includes material deficiencies, tooling performance, and operator capability). Shifts in the process average defective indicate changes in the elements comprising the process capability, and, therefore, constitute a warning that one or more of the process variables has shifted.

Cost-of-Quality Reports

Without the attendant measures of costs it is inordinately difficult to show progress, or lack of it, in a common denominator familiar to all management people. That is why measurement of quality costs is important.

Every business needs two prime measuring sticks to remain a viable enterprise: planned results and actual results. By planning and by comparing actual to planned results, a company is able to chart its course and make the necessary adjustments to plan along the way. Quality assurance is no different. Its function is to establish a quality plan for the company (not just the quality assurance department) and to measure results at significant intervals that allow it to see just how well it is doing according to plan, and to take the necessary steps to correct deviations should they appear from time to time.

Cost-of-quality (COQ) reporting permits this to happen. It has been the best method yet devised to allow a company to plan effectively for quality. And, to my knowledge, it is the best tool yet perfected for keeping a company on the right course once it has embarked on the journey. I do not intend to describe here the mechanics of establishing and maintaining COQ. That has been done already and done well by many other quality practitioners. One has only to read published quality literature to gain a full understanding of the technique.

I would, however, like to share with you some of the shortcuts and pitfalls I discovered while implementing cost-of-quality systems. In a previous chapter I advised having the cost-of-quality report issued by accounting rather than quality assurance so as to establish credibility of the data. This idea has much merit, and should be used *after* the COQ (cost-of-quality) report has been well established, but you will probably find it necessary, at least at the beginning, to dig out the data yourself.

You will find it necessary because initially accounting people will not understand the impact of quality costs and will therefore have a correspondingly small interest in the technique. If your efforts are successful, accounting will eventually publish the report routinely. Until then you may find the atmosphere such that quality people will need to handle the responsibility.

Also, published COQ literature would have you assign quality costs to one of three basic categories: (1) failure costs, (2) appraisal costs, and (3) prevention costs. The reasoning is that a modest investment in prevention costs will yield a larger savings in failure and/or appraisal costs. A major problem associated with this approach is that isolating prevention costs is often inordinately troublesome; its costs are often difficult to extract from other cost data and equally difficult to understand and explain.

I have found that eliminating the prevention category does no harm and may, in fact, enhance the understanding needed by readers to use COQ information properly. The real measure of success is still readily observable—the decrease of failure and appraisal costs when compared with sales dollars. That is the *real* test. Many companies are turning away from measuring-prevention costs because they recognize this, because the data are hard to obtain, and because use of the prevention category often encourages people to play the "numbers games" (moving costs from one account to another account to obtain the desired results).

Finally, when presenting cost (or performance) data it is well to use the Pareto format. In any summation of problems it will be obvious that a small percentage of the problems contributes to a vast share of the total cost and trouble. The Pareto principle helps to isolate and reveal exactly what those problems are. As an example, Table 3 shows the results of a paint shop's analysis of its quality rejections for one day.

Of the total categories of eleven defects the first four contribute 95 percent of the total rejections. Directing full attention to these four will yield far greater results than trying to attack the entire list. Even a mediocre improvement on the

Table 3.

Paint shop's quality rejections on a typical day.

Defect	Defect Costs	Percentage of Total	Cumulative Percentage
1. Dirt in paint	$ 320	32.0	32.0
2. Sags	280	28.0	60.0
3. Dirt	200	20.0	80.0
4. Runs	150	15.0	95.0
5. Off-color	25	2.5	97.5
6. Thin coat	10	1.0	98.5
7. Thin primer	5	0.5	99.0
8. Low impact	4	0.4	99.4
9. Hardness	3	0.3	99.7
10. Bend resistance	2	0.2	99.9
11. Adhesion	1	0.1	100.0
Totals:	$1,000	100.0	

first four types of defects will produce greater results than the complete elimination of the last seven defects.

COQ is a powerful tool in the hands of quality assurance. With it, quality assurance can talk in terms that management understands: dollars and cents, cost, return on investment, and so on. Because the entire business is geared to think this way, the positive effects of quality plans and the negative effects of poor quality can be understood better by the entire organization.

Special Studies

Special studies include one-shot studies on such topics as new tool capability and quality problem analysis and task force reports.

The best thing that can be said about special study reports is that they should be as brief and infrequent as possible. A one-time study of a machine tool's capability can be summarized in a one-page report with detailed backup data going *only* to the people who need the data.

One of the greatest sins of quality assurance professionals is the compulsion to overwhelm with paperwork. Resist the impulse. Your good judgment will tell you when it's needed. Follow your instincts carefully.

9. *Keep Inspection Eyeballs Calibrated*

One of the most basic—and one of the most neglected—facets of quality assurance involves the replication of testing results among different inspection groups. For example, many of the tests performed in a final product surveillance are exactly the same tests performed in-process. Also, two company plants may produce exactly the same product and have the same tests performed in both plants.

Why should this basic need even be mentioned here? Simply because it is so basic that it often is given only the most cursory attention while more sophisticated techniques occupy the organization.

Calibration of eyeballs starts with standardization of test specifications and test equipment, and ends with replication of testing standards. It is common sense to assume that the same product tested in two or more different locations will use the same test specifications and test equipment. In too many cases, this just doesn't happen. Often the responsibility for establishing standardized test specifications and equipment is fuzzy, and the normal result is that each location establishes its own. In other instances selection of standards is left to the imagination of each and every quality assurance supervisor. Again, the results are predictably chaotic.

What, then, are the essential prerequisites for the calibration of eyeballs? Common sense dictates these steps:

1. Make one part of the organization (normally headquarters quality assurance) responsible for publication of test specifications and test equipment drawings.

2. Monitor the organization to assure that each test center is using the same test specifications and test equipment.

3. Do not adopt any proposed changes to the test specifications until the responsible organization has approved and published the changes. At that point, all testing units should incorporate the change.

4. Make one part of the organization responsible for dissemination of visual and written test standards.

5. Use steps 2 and 3 above for application of standards.

6. Do not rely on verbal instructions for application of test standards. Always commit instructions to writing and, whenever possible (particularly with subjective standards, such as paint defects), supply visual aids.

7. Periodically requalify inspectors, using the standards to assure uniformity of inspection among the different stations or plants.

8. See to it that part of the organization responsible for determining test equipment also maintains an active calibration program. Although each individual plant will conduct its own calibration schedule based on master standards, headquarters should monitor results and maintain central records.

10. Budget Traps to Avoid

I have no intention here of showing you how to prepare a budget. Enormous volumes of material written by all sorts of experts have already covered that ground well. Rather, I would like to show you how to avoid two of the common, and sometimes fatal, budgetary traps that plague *all* quality departments. These are best illustrated by actual case histories.

In the first case, I had been engaged by a machinery manufacturer on the eastern seaboard to improve its product quality. Soon after I arrived, it became abundantly clear that not only did product quality need improving, but that if significant moves were not made soon, the company would begin losing sales because of dissatisfied customers. As it was, the percentage of repeat sales (additional sales made to previous customers) had fallen drastically in recent years.

An initial survey of quality activities revealed that all the needed functions were being performed: good design control, proper inspection placement in manufacturing, an active quality engineering function, adequate gauge control, comprehensive performance and quality cost reporting, and so on. In fact, the more I investigated, the more puzzled I became. The quality assurance department appeared to have everything going for it. And yet, machines were falling apart in the customers' plants.

I began looking closely at performance reports to see if I could spot any patterns. Here, once more, there was nothing that could be construed as being unusual. The normal and expected ups and downs and problem areas were clearly apparent. But nowhere could I detect any major pattern of deterioration in product quality.

The machines this company made were installed in customers' plants by servicemen who worked for the company. Since my initial analysis of quality practices in the plant did not reveal significant loopholes, I began to wonder if the servicemen were creating the problems themselves through poor installation procedures. From past experience, I had known that effective quality assurance cannot stop at the shipping platform, but must extend through proper sales and service to the customer. And I had encountered instances in the past in which ineffective service had generated customer complaints, even though the basic products leaving the factory were of high quality.

Before I left for the field, however, I decided to talk to some of the production and quality assurance supervisors in the assembly section of the plant where the machines were assembled and prepared for shipment. I thought an understanding of their problems would enhance my knowledge of specific problems to look for in the field.

I began questioning them, and it wasn't too long before a pattern began to emerge. The assembly supervisors *were* experiencing all manner of product quality problems: defective parts, poor fit of component assemblies, and parts wrongly identified and sent to the subassembly lines. It soon became apparent that the machine shop feeding the assembly floor was, in fact, delivering a substantial quantity of defective parts.

This was puzzling, because machine shop performance reports did not substantiate the poor quality level of parts being made. This disparity triggered a reinvestigation of machine shop quality practices.

The most common defect experienced in assembly was poor hole alignment. I checked the quality performance reports emanating from the drilling department and, much to my surprise, its quality performance index was listed at a high 98.5 percent. Yet products with drilling defects were leaving the machine shop undetected.

A subsequent analysis of inspection procedures in the drilling department finally revealed the basic fault with the quality system. Inspectors were doing the right things, but there weren't enough inspectors to do the job properly. They were spread so thin, attempting to cover first-piece inspection, patrol inspection, and tollgate (final lot) inspection, that they could not do justice to all of them. Sample plans were being aborted while inspectors frantically, but ineffectively, attempted to cover all bases.

A little more digging revealed the sad story. The condition noted in drilling was, in fact, prevalent throughout the machine shop. Management was attempting, once again, to reduce labor costs without analyzing its effects. Actually, costs were higher for the company because inspectors were not able to perform their jobs adequately. But the controller was happy, simply because he thought he was holding the line on indirect labor costs in the machine shop. He did not look further. And the quality assurance manager was equally culpable, because he had made no analysis that would indicate in hard dollars the deceptively easy road but costly effects of that type of shortsighted control.

Unfortunately, that type of thinking is prevalent, particularly among financial men and hard-driving, cost-conscious manufacturing executives. Yet one of the primary jobs of the quality assurance manager is to let these people know, in stentorian tones, if need be, the drastic and foolish results that can be anticipated. It is his job to counteract short-term savings at the expense of product quality.

That is the first budgetary trap to be avoided.

The second can best be illustrated by an experience I had with a pharmaceutical company in New Jersey. This company had a receiving inspection activity that sampled inspected goods received from company suppliers as well as from outside vendors. The company also had a financial vice-president who wanted to eliminate all inspections (and, of course, inspectors) devoted to sampling goods from internal company suppliers on the grounds that the company supplier (another plant) had already inspected the goods.

I hadn't been on board with this company for two days as a consultant when I was called into the financial vice-president's office and given the opportunity to hear his case. Trying to be as objective as possible, I told him I would investigate the merits of his suggestion and let him know what I thought of it.

It didn't take too long to verify that the incoming quality level of the company suppliers was *lower* than the quality level of outside vendors. And it wasn't too long after my investigation that I convinced him of the folly of his suggestion.

Let's put this issue in perspective. Every company has two potential sources of supply: internal and external suppliers. Much has been written in management literature about outside vendor control, but very little about the relations between supplier and user factories in the same company.

There is good reason for this. It is generally assumed that an internal—but separate—plant is just like another department in the user factory. Nothing could be further from the truth. The supplier plant is a separate profit center with its own set of unique problems. These are compounded by geographical separation from the user factory. Communications and exchange of information become a problem because of the separation. Remember, the supplier factory is subject to the same outside problems any supplier has: imperfections in manufacturing and design, imperfections in the quality system, and shipping damage.

Frequently, financial people seriously question the need for one plant checking semifinished product from a supplier plant within the same company. It is a facile target and the financial people see a large dollar savings realized by eliminating the receiving inspection function entirely. Unfortunately the savings will be short-lived. The quality budget undoubtedly will look great for the short run, but manufacturing rejections due to defective vendor material normally more than offset the savings realized through elimination of the inspection function.

It makes sense to handle an in-company vendor with at least as much care as you would any outside vendor. When he ships you new products, you inspect more thoroughly; when his products show a continuous record of high quality, you lighten the inspections; and when his goods show signs of quality slippage, you zoom in hard and try to correct the problem before it gets out of hand.

Certain key phrases used by financial and manufacturing people should alert the quality practitioner to bad times coming. These phrases herald a hue and cry either to cut inspectors from the workforce or to spread them too thin. Typical examples are:

• "First-piece inspection and final inspection aren't enough. We want you to check the jobs while they're running, too. Of course, you'll have to do this without adding any inspectors."

• "We don't need any inspectors in assembly. Let's eliminate their jobs and let the operators inspect their own work. Think of the money we'll save."

• "I don't really understand why you have a final product inspection before shipment. After all, you've inspected the products in-process. Why is it necessary to check them again? Can't you do the job right the first time?"

• "If you made our vendors step up to their responsibilities we wouldn't need any receiving inspection, would we?"

• "I don't understand why you need so many inspectors. I just visited our plant in Germany, and I'll bet it only has about half the inspectors we have."

• "If you used statistical quality control, I'll bet you could reduce your inspectors by 25 percent."

Finally, remember this. It is all too easy to look like a hero by consistently operating below budget. It's particularly easy in quality assurance. All you need do is cut some essential service. But it will catch up with you in high scrap and rework costs and, worse, dissatisfied customers. Your job is to blend all the essential ingredients of quality and, as a result, keep customers happy. If you do that job, and do it well, quality-associated costs will be minimized. Look to your cost-of-quality report to tell the story. But don't just listen to the financial men and do what they expect.

11. How to Set Up a Products Liability Program

Not too long ago when a dissatisfied customer had a gripe against a product, chances were he would make an angry telephone call or write a nasty letter to the president of the company that sold the product. Not today. Now the customer calls one of the many flourishing products liability attorneys and starts a lawsuit.

During the past several years, the concept of liability has undergone drastic change. The principle of strict liability at one time placed the burden of proof on the injured party. Today that condition has effectively been reversed by the courts. Now, strict liability is construed as compensation to the injured party regardless of responsibility or negligence. The "fault" system, therefore, has been replaced by the "no fault" system. Today the plaintiff in a lawsuit has only to prove that his injury was caused by a product. He does not need to prove that the manufacturer's design is faulty. Nor does he need to prove carelessness in manufacturing.

Today, a manufacturer can lose literally millions of dollars in a *single* case, depending on the circumstances. And its employees might find themselves personally liable for damages resulting from poor decisions they made. Even if their skirts are clean, liability insurance premiums alone can, and have, put some companies out of business. Premium increases for some manufacturers have increased as much as 1,000 percent, while other, less fortunate companies have flatly been refused insurance coverage.

To some extent, therefore, a company's future may rest on its ability to establish a realistic products liability program. When I was a quality assurance manager for a large capital goods manufacturer on the East Coast, I started a products liability program that was regarded by its insurance carrier as a model program. It included four elements:

1. A statement of corporate policy regarding products liability.
2. A products liability steering committee.
3. A product engineering safety task force that reported to the products liability steering committee.
4. A products liability claim defense program.

Each of these elements will now be examined in detail.

The Corporate Policy Statement

The purpose here is to create a guiding policy similar in intent to the corporate quality policy. It directs top management's attention to the products liability problem and provides a philosophy to handle the problem. The framework is set to establish standards and controls.

A corporate policy for products liability can run anywhere from one to several pages, depending on the level of detail addressed in the policy. A central statement, however, forms the nucleus of intent, and an example is given here:

The company will provide customers with safe products and services. Company programs will be developed and implemented that ensure that all products and services are safe for their intended and reasonable forseeable use; that they perform their required functions safely, reliably, and with minimum effects on environment; that they comply with applicable governmental laws and regulations; that they meet or exceed industry and governmental standards; and that they offer minimal risk or injury to personnel and damage to property.

The company is committed to assure that these objectives are attained through the implementation of safety procedures and methods in engineering design, product development, manufacturing, promotion, advertising, sales, and service.

Some policies go on to address responsibilities for each of the areas mentioned above specifically. An option is to have the products liability steering committee spell out all the responsibilities. Any products liability policy issued should have prior approval of the company's legal department.

The Products Liability Steering Committee

This committee, which has the job of discharging the responsibilities defined in the corporate policy statement, should have the following company representation: quality assurance; marketing (sales, service, advertising); manufacturing (production, purchasing, manufacturing, engineering); product engineering; the legal department; and administration (financial and insurance).

Normally, quality assurance should chair the committee. From an insurance carrier's point of view (and its view is the important one—it is supplying the insurance coverage) the chairman should be from a department with the broadest possible viewpoint. Since quality assurance has no vested interest in the results of functional areas, its contribution should be the most objective (particularly if it reports to general management rather than, say, manufacturing or product engineering). The chairman should report his findings and be responsible to the president of the company.

The products liability committee should be held responsible for the successful implementation and maintenance of the products liability program. A plan should be developed and installed, and the committee should meet regularly to review progress. Its charter is to assure progress of the program, to listen to and advise on safety problems reported in-house and in the field (customers), to ensure dedication to the program, and to discuss recent developments in the products liability field.

The steering committee must provide answers to the following type of questions:

- How are recurring safety and quality problems handled?
- How are customer complaints handled?
- Who approves promotional literature and advertising, and what guidelines do they use?
- How are vendors' materials and parts inspected and what acceptance records are maintained?
- How are manufacturing operations inspected and what acceptance records are maintained?
- What degree of traceability is needed from the finished product in customers' hands back to raw materials and components?
- Who has the responsibility for implementing product safety improvements?
- Are adequate records maintained of:
    Designs and drawing changes?
    Sales and service contracts?
    Claims?
    All product literature?
    Recalls?
    Packaging and shipping records?

The Product Engineering Safety Task Force

Subordinate to the products liability steering committee, this task force has the responsibility for studying company products, making appropriate changes in design, and, where appropriate, providing warning signs on the product. Generally, the product engineering safety task force is composed of product engineering representatives, and its chairman serves as a member of the products liability steering committee. Its agenda and recommendations are usually approved by the steering committee.

When product engineering evaluates the safety features of a product, it must be able to answer questions like these:

- Is the product fit for all forseeable uses? Can it cause accidents or injuries?
- Has the product been designed to minimize injuries?
- Are there adequate warning signs on the product cautioning against possible inherent dangers?
- Does the product conform to or exceed established government and association standards?
- Does the procedure have the latest state-of-the-art design?
- Have safeguards been incorporated within the design?
- Does the product meet specified reliability levels?
- Are installation, operation, and maintenance manuals complete and easily understandable?

The Products Liability Claim Defense Program

The objective of the program is to produce a defect-free, totally safe product, just as the objective of the quality program should be to produce the best quality product on the market. Both are ideals, but the closer the company comes to both goals, the better prepared it is to prevent products liability losses.

Each segment of the company must contribute to the

products liability program. The following general steps are needed:

Product Design. The approach to minimizing products liability losses through design has been discussed. Products must be designed in full compliance with all laws, codes, and regulations. These may come from government sources, industry standards, and company specifications. Product engineers must also consider all possible ways the product could be used and misused.

Protective devices, guards, warning signs, and safety instructions *must always* accompany the product.

Manufacturing Testing. The final quality and safety of the product are often direct results of the manufacturing processes. These processes can be chemical formulations, fabrication, machining, heat treating, plating, painting, and a large range of other operations. Control of the equipment, tooling, and operator methods, among others, will determine, in part, the quality and safety of the finished product. Always make sure gauges and testing equipment are calibrated and traceable to the National Bureau of Standards tolerances. Inspection systems cannot be relied upon when testing devices do not meet recognized standards.

Quality Assurance. Every product leaving the plant must be subjected to complete and effective testing programs. All tests must be written and monitored. Also, all tests should be recorded and maintained carefully throughout the life of the product.

The same quality methodologies applied to internal product testing must be applied, just as thoroughly, to vendors' products.

Good quality assurance records are an important line of defense in the event of a claim.

Product Manuals and Instructions. Properly designed and prepared manuals and instructions not only help the customer use the product, they also educate him about the *proper* use of the product. If the customer is unaware of possible limitations and dangers of the product, a company can find itself virtually defenseless if an injury occurs.

Product manuals and instructions should, among other things:

- Contain the needed information to assemble, use, and maintain the product safely.
- Contain a parts list and installation instructions.
- Explain operation and maintenance procedures that will keep the product safe and fit for foreseeable use.
- Advise of product uses, limitations, possible hazards, and results of misuse.
- Recommend emergency actions in the event of a failure.
- Warn against modifying the product or replacing failed or worn parts with inferior components.

Sales and Service Literature. Advertising, promotional material, service contracts, brochures, manuals, and any other information given to customers and users should be reviewed carefully by product engineering, marketing, and company lawyers before issuance. Words and phrases may misrepresent the ability of a product to meet customer expectations or they may overstate the ability of a product's capability to perform.

Photographs used in any disseminated literature should promote the safe and proper use of the product.

Packaging and Shipping. Potential storage, handling, and shipping hazards should be explained carefully to all people from factory to customer who handle the product. Containers should always be designed to assure safe handling throughout the distribution cycle. Appropriate labels must indicate contents clearly.

Finally, before you attempt to establish a products liability program, contact your company legal people for guidelines. The worst possible thing to do is to proceed on your own without their advice.

Chapter V

Professionalizing Quality Management

I know of no more encouraging fact than the unquestionable ability of man to elevate his life by a conscious endeavor.

—HENRY DAVID THOREAU

1. Be a Businessman

If you're in quality assurance today, you have one of the toughest, most demanding jobs going. Not only are you battered on all sides in traditional style by production, engineering, and sales, but now you're also subject to the increasingly strident demands of consumer groups and a knowledgeable, sophisticated public. On top of this, a proliferation of regulatory bodies is forcing you to absorb and implement a multitude of sometimes contradictory laws and regulations. And, if that's not enough, someone's already whispering in your ear about the forthcoming change to metric measurement. All in all, it's a tough and relentless environment—an environment needing all the skills you can muster just to survive.

Unfortunately, survival in this kind of atmosphere is no easy matter. On the contrary, it has become more and more difficult to remain on the job. Many quality practitioners, sensing this, have tended to drift toward the more sophisticated, higher-technology techniques at the expense of basic, commonsense methodologies that have ably supported them on the job. As we have seen, this is no criticism. Most technical people are so oriented. And the new technology can often benefit the organization. But the recent advances in technology have drawn us further and further away from the realities of getting a job done, and that, all too frequently, has resulted in loss of effectiveness on the job.

There is a natural tendency for quality assurance people to be attracted to the technical side of business. After all, they normally have been drafted from the engineering or scientific arms of the company, and their education has been technical. They are, therefore, more susceptible to the dangers of in-

156

terpreting their experiences from restricted viewpoints and deriving conclusions that, from a total business point of view, can best be described as "limited."

Be Results Oriented

How can you avoid that syndrome? Truthfully, the answer isn't simple. If you've been conditioned to filter your experiences and react in a certain way repeatedly for many years, it becomes exceedingly difficult to change your orientation and to react to those same experiences in a different fashion. If you're to think as a businessman, however, you must master that technique. But how can you best reorient your approach?

Probably the quickest and surest way is to focus on results. Before embarking on any major change or major program, ask yourself questions like: "How will this affect sales or profits? How will this change contribute to company ROI goals?"

In other words, think like a businessman, not like a technical specialist. Define the role of quality in terms of overall company objectives. Don't allow the dazzle of technical expertise to blind you to the realities of business life. Evaluate your function in terms of dollars and cents, customer satisfaction, and contribution to sales.

Set plans and objectives, and measure their attainment in measurable yardsticks. Evaluate the success of quality efforts by reduction of the company's cost of quality. Focus your efforts on achieving customer satisfaction and measure your effectiveness on the basis of that satisfaction.

Remember that statistics and other mathematical scientific tools are nothing more than a means to an end. Their only function is to help get the job done. The fanciest, most sophisticated analytical method is only as good as its ability to get results in the most economical and efficient manner. If a simpler state-of-the-art technique will do a better job, use it. It's cheaper. Abandon the fancier, but more appealing, method and follow the shortest path to accomplishment. If you fall in love with the fancier method, you have discarded the mantle of results and your performance will suffer for it.

How Not to Do a Job

A business acquaintance told me about the time he was assigned by his company as director of quality assurance for the company's commercial electronics division. When he arrived at the division, he found a plethora of talent available in the form of 22 quality engineers, 130 inspectors, and a sizable quality management staff. The previous director of quality assurance had been a brilliant but highly volatile and disorganized Ph.D. He was one of those rare individuals who had mastered electronic theory, an insightful scientist who was eons ahead of the nearest person in his field.

Unfortunately, he was no businessman. Product quality was significantly below the level of the company's chief competitors, quality costs were skyrocketing, morale in the department was low, and turnover was high. On the other hand, knowledge of state-of-the-art techniques was high and the department owned the newest and most sophisticated and expensive testing equipment.

As my business acquaintance related, the quality department excelled in technical expertise but did not or could not relate its purpose to company profitability. Technical involvement became the goal. Common sense was discarded. Because of that, people were confused and unhappy. They were not accomplishing their mission, and company management continually expressed its dissatisfaction with the quality assurance department.

When the ax fell and my friend replaced the former director, the momentum and sense of direction improved immediately. Goals were established consistent with company objectives, solid plans were laid, and the organization became geared and motivated to achieve product quality improvements.

Within a matter of months, product quality levels increased significantly and, concurrently, quality costs were reduced. In no time after that, it was discovered the department could function best with only 12 engineers and 90 inspectors. All this, mind you, with significant improvements in the quality level.

The Quality Assurance Businessman

There are certain elements of professionalism common to quality assurance organizations that conduct their operations in a businesslike fashion. Here is a distillation of the most significant of them:

• Quality policy is defined. The policy document delineates the company's commitment to its product quality position in the field and in the factory. It describes the standards and levels of achievement the company considers necessary to satisfy customers and, at the same time, operate the factory (or business) within specified quality costs.

• Using the company quality policy as a guideline, specific plans of product quality achievement are specified. Performance goals are set for customer satisfaction, finished product, scrap, rework, receiving inspection, and other relevant operations.

• Cost-of-quality and performance reports (batch acceptance, process average defective, and so on) are established for each of the areas just described.

• The reports are used to spot high-cost, poor-performance areas, allowing the organization to focus on those areas most in need of improvement.

• All areas of the company participate in the quality plan:

marketing, manufacturing, engineering, finance, and personnel. Specific goals are established, aimed at achieving customer satisfaction for all operating areas. Without this total involvement there can be no true balance between the vital factors of customer satisfaction and profitability. Something will be lacking. The company will not be getting the most for its money.

2. The KISS Technique

Several years ago, when I had just finished graduate school, I became a member of the quality engineering department of a large medical products company. My newfound knowledge of linear programming, decision trees, regression analysis, and other sophisticated tools was burning a hole in my pocket—I was itching to apply each of them in the worst way.

There were several quality engineers with recent graduate degrees and each of them, like myself, was searching out opportunities to observe his education in action (and, of course, the chance to impress our peers and bosses). Merrily we went on our separate ways, implanting seeds of knowledge wherever we wandered. It wasn't too long before we had managed, in our eagerness to apply the latest technological systems and methods, to mess things up royally.

About that time the chief quality engineer called us into his conference room. No reason was given for the meeting and as we awaited the chief's arrival we were all visibly nervous. Finally the conference room door opened and the chief quality engineer walked in. Without saying a word to any of us he walked directly to the blackboard, picked up a piece of chalk, and wrote these letters:

KISS

He then pivoted around and stared hard and long at each of us in turn. During those tense moments not a word was said. Some of us were already sweating, and every one of us felt deep down that, for whatever reason imaginable, we were on our last legs. The utterly serious and stern demeanor of our boss convinced us we were about to be fired.

The chief cleared his throat and asked "Do any of you what the acronym KISS means?" Nobody knew, and nobody dared say a word. His question was greeted with absolute silence. He then turned toward the blackboard and wrote:

KEEP IT SIMPLE, STUPID

With that done, he laid down the chalk, dusted off his hands, and walked directly out of the room without saying another word. His exit was marked only by the stunned expressions on our faces.

It's a lesson I'll never forget. The chief was something of a dramatist, and he wanted to get his point across emphatically. Needless to say, he didn't miss the target. In his own way he wanted to teach us what our swollen egos were almost incapable of absorbing—that our technical razzle-dazzle wasn't getting the job done; that the best way to do something is always the simplest way possible under the circumstances.

An urge to complicate exists today, particularly among technical specialists. The more technical the demands of the job, the greater the urge to complicate festers. Product engineers, scientists, statisticians, quality practitioners, and a multitude of other specialists suffer from this disease. Few are immune.

Quality assurance, with a history of technical orientation, is no less enamored of the scientific approach than its engineering brethren. Actually, there are times when it seems more immersed in technical razzle-dazzle than anybody else in the company, particularly when statistical jargon starts flying.

We have examined (in Chapter I) the reasons for that phenomenon and have discovered that the evolution of quality assurance can be defined in technical terms. Its education and experience have been limited. That is the reason many quality managers feel more comfortable tackling a product problem instead of a "people" problem. And that is the reason they sometimes feel more at home with scientific facts than with subjective judgments.

Many of them have that seemingly endless compulsion to make everything difficult by relying on scientific tools instead of practical methods. Rather than train a machine operator to do a quality job, they would prefer to install a convoluted statistical sampling plan on the operator's machine. Rather than discuss customer problems with a group of salesmen and distributors, they would be happier working on those same problems in the test laboratory, establishing a testing protocol.

There is, in other words, a massive urge to steer away from the simple and direct approach and, instead, focus on superficial and less productive issues. The customer's problems, for example, won't be solved until those problems are defined, and that takes face-to-face contact. Designing a test protocol is part of the procedure to eliminate the problem, but it is a minor and easier one by comparison.

People in all occupational groups respond more promptly and with more understanding when the instructions they receive are readily comprehendible. When nontechnical people must rely on technical direction, the danger of cloudy communications is ever-present. The technical person, opting to use technical methods alone to solve the problems, must first show subordinates what to do and how to do it. The chances are high, under those circumstances, that subordinates will make serious errors because they lack a basic understanding of the technology.

Quality practitioners who heed the compulsion to complicate things should always remember the acronym KISS. It can do wonders in realigning the thought processes. KISS helps everyone zero in on that which is direct and meaningful and fosters an aversion for that which confuses.

3. The Need for Discipline and Direction

For several reasons, quality assurance has often had a poor image with other departments in the company. Frequently complaints have been voiced about inspectors being lazy, goofing off, not holding to budgets, not caring about meeting delivery schedules, not understanding cost imperatives, and committing a multitude of other sins.

It would do us well to remember that where there is smoke, there is fire. Although many of the complaints have been unjustified, enough are founded in fact to create resentments, and the reputation of the quality department has been hurt. Once people sour on a department, they tend to withdraw support from its efforts (a fatal situation for quality assurance).

Quality assurance generally is not subjected to the same measurements of efficiency as manufacturing departments. Performance, utilization, productivity—these are tools of control over production, but they have seldom been applied to quality assurance.

As a consequence, the manufacturing departments—where quality assurance is most visible through its inspectors—have been forced to discipline themselves to survive and to be successful. But since quality assurance people are seldom subjected to those same disciplines, other than by osmosis, they are not as well disciplined. Therefore, too few people (in uncontrolled or loosely controlled cases) adhere religiously to budgets or pay close attention to costs.

The astute quality manager can instill the needed discipline through careful direction and the application of fundamentals. These are:

1. *Write a Quality Plan and Live by It.* Goals for warranty, customer complaints, competitive quality position, cost of quality, or other *quantitative* measures should be established, along with a plan of action to achieve those goals. Then, quality assurance must be disciplined to live by its commitments to the plan.

2. *Stay Within Budget.* A department that can accomplish its goals and stay within budget is respected by top management and other departments alike. Having them learn to stay within budget is also a great way to teach quality supervisors the value of costs.

3. *Keep Head Counts in Line.* There is nothing more discouraging for a production supervisor than having to run a tight ship while observing an excess of people in quality assurance. An effective quality manager will gear his head count (salaried supervisors and inspectors alike) to productive projects only and learn how to run a lean organization.

4. *Respect Delivery Schedules.* Nothing is more frustrating to a manufacturing person or salesman than the nonchalant attitude some quality assurance people display regarding delivery schedules. Quality assurance must recognize the importance of delivering products to customers on time, and that message must be felt throughout the organization. Quality supervisors must demonstrate their willingness to provide quick—but thorough—inspection services when warranted.

5. *Participate in Cost Reduction Projects.* Any criticism for lack of cost consciousness directed against quality assurance will evaporate when it displays its willingness to participate vigorously in cost reduction projects. One of the most common criticisms directed against quality assurance has been its seeming lack of interest in reducing costs. That criticism is largely disappearing today as quality assurance is spearheading scrap and refinish cost reduction efforts and participating in other company-sponsored cost reduction activities.

6. *Display a Sense of Urgency.* This about sums it up. A contributing quality practitioner will understand the necessity of making a profit and will act accordingly.

4. Play the Devil's Advocate

Playing the devil's advocate is one of the most difficult yet necessary roles of quality assurance. Someone, when new products and processes are introduced, must ask, "What can go wrong?" and must investigate every detail thoroughly with that thought in mind. His job is not to say what can go right, but rather to determine what can go wrong and then do whatever needs to be done to prevent it.

Because the role of devil's advocate has a negative connotation, most people will shy away from taking it on and asking the necessary questions. Of course, when nobody in the organization scrutinizes the details, there is bound to be trouble later on down the road. Either somebody forgot some important detail or somebody did something wrong, or both.

Unfortunately, and this happens too many times, the quality assurance person who conscientiously asks those embarrassing questions is ridiculed and accused of negativism. The questioning of detail is often abhorrent, for example, to the marketing person who wants to push ahead with the new product at all costs—and damn the petty details.

The rather imposing job of the quality practitioner, under these circumstances, is to persevere in as positive a fashion as possible, explaining his role as one that will contribute substantially to advancement of the total project. It might be readily apparent, for example, that some supposedly minor detail could hold up the project indefinitely unless it is soon resolved. But it cannot be resolved before it is brought to the surface—and that is customarily the job of quality assurance.

A friend of mine, a former quality manager for a medical products company, recalls the time his company was struggling to introduce a new product that was considered a major advance in the medical field. He recognized the importance to his company of manufacturing and selling the new product successfully. He also recognized that the product was not developed enough to manufacture successfully on a day-in, day-out basis. Quality engineering had predicted a failure rate of 20 percent. Translated into dollars and cents, that wiped out any profit for the new product. It was also acknowledged that at the projected failure rate, it would be exceedingly difficult to contain all defective product in the factory and in fact, there would be a high failure rate in customers' hands. The defective product would not result in injuries, but it would create a bad image for the company in an industry for which product excellence is critical.

Nevertheless, the quality manager was hesitant to voice his doubts. He griped about the problem to his boss, but he did nothing to question the product engineering and marketing men who were jamming the product through channels to completion. He was, quite frankly, afraid. The need of his company for new products, coupled with the drive of the marketing organization to get a salable product in the field, discouraged any open criticism of the product. A person who dared voice his true feelings would be publicly condemned by marketing and product engineering as a "negative thinker." An atmosphere of fear enveloped the project.

Shortly after product introduction, customer complaints overwhelmed management. The inevitable witch-hunt ensued, and the quality manager was held responsible, at least in top management's eyes, for permitting a low-quality product to reach the field. The manager was astute enough to recognize that he was "damned if he did, and damned if he didn't" but recognized too late that he should have blown the whistle before the product reached the field. Taking his lumps at that time would have been infinitely preferable to taking them after the fiasco had occurred. It was somebody else's goof before the product was shipped, but afterward, the error belonged to the quality manager *alone.*

Remember: You can close your eyes to an unpleasant fact and avoid an unpleasant confrontation during the planning and implementation phases. But when the product reaches the field and fails in the customer's hands, it's your baby—not the design engineer who made an error in a critical tolerance or the chemist who made a terrible mistake in the original formulation. Management is looking at *you.* And invariably it's going to ask one horribly embarrassing question: "How did you let this get into the field?" Regardless of what happens inside the factory, once you have allowed the product to go out into the marketplace, it is yours, 100 percent yours. That's worth considering, isn't it?

5. Keep in Contact with the Firing Line

Talk to different people at different levels of the organization. The story you get from the operator on the line may not even faintly resemble those beautifully prepared graphs on prominent display in your office. And don't confine yourself to the factory. Speak to people in the distributor's showroom and repair shop, the vendor's manufacturing line, the service department, design engineering, production engineering, and so on.

Certainly I'm not advocating spending any given percentage of your time on the floor. That depends entirely on your place and role in the organization. If you're a quality assurance foreman, chances are you spend 90 percent of your time on the floor. Conversely, if you're two steps higher on the ladder, say a quality assurance manager, your exposure to the "line of fire" is considerably less. And that's the danger. The higher you are in any organization the further you're removed from the truth. You become insulated simply because the events of the day are filtered to you through three or four organizational layers. Since the interpretations that people give to any event will vary, depending on motivation and comprehension, the version you hear usually misses by varying degrees what actually happened.

The only effective way to find out what's really happening is to do it firsthand. Get out of your office and visit the combat area. Talk to as many people as possible, get all the prevailing views, then determine for yourself what's really going on.

Naturally, you don't want to verify every piece of information that crosses your desk. That would take forever. What you should do, however, is determine what it is you need to know, consider the source of information, and then go and see for yourself if you're unsure about the source. If you don't adopt this technique or one similar to it, chances are that sooner or later you will make the wrong decisions based on the wrong information, and wind up accomplishing nothing and becoming ineffective on the job.

6. *Product Quality Presentations*

Let's face it. Image making, publicity, and selling have not been strong suits of quality practitioners. Most members of the profession are technically oriented specialists who have had neither the time nor the inclination to make successful pitches for product quality. They are not advertising men or publicity agents. That whole scene is foreign to them; they just do not feel *comfortable* selling their wares.

And this has been one of the major failings of the profession.

Look at it this way: To make the importance of product quality known, people must be educated to realize the potential of both good and bad product quality. All capable quality assurance people understand the value of quality—profit contribution and repeat sales. They also are fully cognizant of the unhappy results of poor quality—high costs and loss of sales.

Yet many members of management may *not* really be aware of the awesome contribution (positive or negative) that quality may have on their products. Normally, their attention has been devoted to producing, costing, designing, selling, and servicing the product. Their day-to-day commitment to increasing sales levels and getting out the work is often over-whelming and simply does not leave them time to give adequate consideration to product quality (Take it or leave it, that's the way things have been, whether we like it or not.) Neither has labor given the attention to product quality that it so fully deserves. Labor has been subject to the same pressures that motivate its bosses.

It is therefore reasonable to assume that the quality practitioner must be the person who first makes the quality case known. Not too many others will have the same knowledge and motivation. One of the best methods of acquainting both management and labor with the quality story is through the annual product quality presentation, which tells how the company's quality fared over the past year. It is a persuasive way of capturing an audience and making a sales pitch. No other format I have used has had such an impact. It gives you the chance to tailor the story to selected audiences and get some vital messages across. It almost invariably results in help given to achieve quality goals, whether that help comes from management, labor, or both.

Certain essential ingredients are needed for a successful product quality presentation:

Type of Presentation. A slide presentation is generally more effective than use of an overhead projector or hand-drawn charts on an easel. Slides are more attractive, and using them in sequence permits a smooth flow of pictures and graphs.

Maximum Time. Never exceed one hour. People bore eas-ily, regardless of whether they occupy seats in the executive suite or operate milling machines in the factory. Taking too much time buries salient features in superfluous material. The discipline of using only a minimum of time forces you to make your points simply and effectively.

Audience. The more people that understand the problems and goals of quality, the easier the job of the quality assurance manager. It is best, however, not to mix audiences. For example, when I have made annual quality results presentations, I have made them to the following audiences in order of appearance:

Board of directors and upper management
Quality assurance (supervisors *and* inspectors)
Middle management—*all* departments
First line supervision
Outlying plants—domestic and overseas

I have used the same presentation but, obviously, the questions and discussion have varied, depending on the composition of the audience.

Frequency. This presentation is probably best given annually, for two good reasons. First, too much exposure bores people, and second, the time needed to prepare a talk of this nature is extensive.

Number of Speakers. I have found that it is best to include each plant quality assurance manager, each of them presenting the quality story for his area of responsibility. Preparation of the talk allows each participant to think carefully about his section's results for the past year and goals for the coming year.

Best Time for Presentation. Certainly, don't make your presentation immediately after a social hour and dinner. Regardless of the interest of the audience, the drinks and food will overcome it. It is my experience that an optimum time is first thing in the morning, when everybody is fresh, relaxed, and attentive. If the presentation is made in the evening, do it before cocktails. This helps assure attentiveness.

Order of Presentation. Use the same order of presentation that parallels the flow of work in your business: vendor liaison, receiving inspection, process control, finished product testing, and last, but most important, field results and cost of quality. The latter can be warranty, number of field complaints of customer dissatisfaction surveys, or other quality-cost indicators. Field results will show the culmination of the quality effort, and if the job has been done properly, it will show improving product quality in customers' hands and reduced cost of quality.

Format. For each of the areas just described, the following information will be of major interest:

1. Results should be shown, using lot and/or piece acceptance criteria in graphs that show comparative annual data.

2. Major problems and major accomplishments should be discussed briefly.

3. Goals for the coming year should be highlighted, along with the reasons for setting specific goals and a description of the means for achieving them.

Types of Graphs. I have participated in, and observed, many presentations. Experience has illustrated that the simplest graphs give the best results. If you make one point clearly in a graph, and leave it uncluttered, all types of audiences will grasp *and retain* your conclusions. Believe it or not, vice-presidents are not any more likely to understand a complicated graph than foremen are. For example, compare the two graphs in Figure 10 and decide for yourself which one makes its point more distinctly and dramatically.

7. *Shipping Garbage*

A close friend of mine related this experience to me:

I had just been hired as quality manager for a machinery manufacturer in the Midwest. The company was having severe product quality problems, and not only were quality costs high, but repeat

FIGURE 10.
Types of graphs.

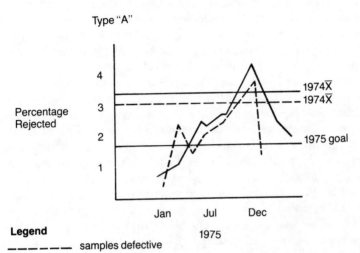

Type "A"

Percentage Rejected

1974$\overline{X}$
1974$\overline{X}$
1975 goal

Jan   Jul   Dec

Legend

1975

– – – – – – samples defective

—————— lots defective

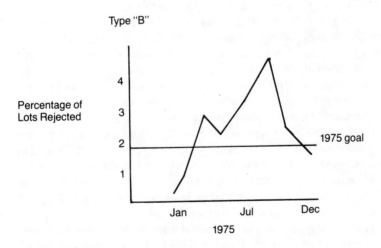

Type "B"

Percentage of Lots Rejected

1975 goal

Jan   Jul   Dec

1975

sales were being lost because of customer disgust with product quality.

I hadn't been with the company for more than a month when it became readily apparent quality assurance was deliberately not inspecting for many important quality characteristics. This condition was prevalent in most operations, but particularly in the assembly department, the final operation before shipment.

When I asked the quality supervisors why they were missing inspections, they all answered that this was a hard-nosed production-oriented company, and that anybody causing missed shipments would get his can thrown out the door. When I talked with the manufacturing manager he gave me more of the same folderol. He ominously recited what had happened to previous quality managers when they had unilaterally decided to hold the line. The manufacturing manager went on to say that my cooperation was essential to get machines shipped, and that product quality was good anyway. He placed the blame for customer quality complaints on faulty service, stupid customers, bad specifications; in fact, everything except manufacturing, which he considered exemplary.

The warning was quite clear. Either continue shipping garbage or start looking for a new job. During my orientation the first week on the job I had been warned this would happen, not only by my people, but by managers in marketing and research. Apparently everybody knew it was happening, but nobody had ever confronted the situation and done anything about it. All the managers commiserated with me, and I could read in their eyes the thought that "Here's another poor guy who'll never make it."

Both the manufacturing manager and myself worked for the same boss, the vice-president of manufacturing, who had hired me. I decided to take the direct approach. I figured the worst thing that could happen was that I would be fired, and I might as well test the possibility of that at the outset. I realized that if I succumbed to the manufacturing manager I would be in his hip pocket for as long as I continued working for the company.

One Friday afternoon, I gathered the assembly quality supervisors and inspectors and instructed them to begin checking for *all* quality characteristics beginning the following Monday morning. When I told them I would not tolerate anybody deliberately letting garbage pass, they were amazed. You could actually see the shock register on their faces. But I meant it, and I convinced my people I was serious. I told them that I would deal personally with anybody who challenged our right to do the job the way it must be done. And I made sure they understood the importance of letting me know when anybody started putting pressure on them to release unacceptable units. I convinced them their jobs would be easier; in effect I was taking the tough decisions out of their hands and assuming the full burden of fighting it out with people challenging our prerogatives.

After they returned to their jobs I went to the manufacturing manager's office and told him the very same thing. I assured him that quality assurance would do its best to remain fair and impartial but that we had no intention of ever again accepting a product that we knew would cause customer dissatisfaction.

His immediate reaction was one of shock. Never before in his ten-year tenure as manufacturing manager had any quality assurance person ever had the audacity to stand up and be counted. It was a new experience for him.

His shock quickly turned to outrage and in a trembling voice he made every veiled threat conceivable, not only on my job but on my physical well-being as well. I stood there and took it, not blinking an eye. I had prepared myself for an onslaught, and it's a good thing I did. Otherwise I might have decked him, and that's exactly what he wanted me to do. It would have cost me my job.

At one point I finally turned around and left his office; left him fuming and sputtering behind me. I went home and, as you can imagine, I had a bad weekend, waiting for Monday and dreading it. It may have taken a lot of guts to take a stand, but I was scared silly that come Monday morning there would be a confrontation and I would be the loser. After all, the manufacturing manager had survived four quality managers over the last ten years, and I was afraid I would be number five.

Monday came and went. The inspectors began checking all the quality characteristics and defect levels rose only slightly. Nobody in manufacturing said a damn thing to quality assurance and the whole day was quiet and uneventful.

Tuesday was another matter altogether. Right away, at 7:00 A.M., the start of the shift, reject levels on the main assembly line began rising alarmingly. By 10:30 A.M. there were so many rejected units the line shut down. Production supervisors were fretting and moaning, but still nobody asked quality assurance to approve the garbage and ship it to customers.

At 11:00 A.M. the manufacturing manager made his long-awaited appearance. He came storming out to the main assembly line, his face so red I thought he was about to burst. But then an unusual and unexpected thing happened. Rather than aiming his wrath directly at inspectors or their supervisors, the manufacturing manager began yelling at his own managers and foremen. He traveled up and down the assembly line chewing out all his people, berating them for doing such a lousy job.

Boy, I never saw such fast action before. Those production guys really started hustling. It wasn't two or three hours before the defect rate was cut about 80 percent. For the balance of the shift quality levels remained high. Shortly after going through his act, the manufacturing manager had returned to his office.

Quality levels not only held for the balance of the week, they actually improved. It didn't take anybody long to figure out that quality assurance was *not* going to be challenged by the manufacturing manager. As soon as his attitude became obvious, it reached down to every level of the production organization.

Within weeks positive attitudes replaced irresponsible practices. Manufacturing and quality assurance began cooperating with each other instead of fighting each other. Improvements began to be obvious. The whole atmosphere had totally flip-flopped.

An interesting experience, isn't it? How many of *you* have been in the exact same predicament? It's really only the very few in quality assurance who haven't faced that situation repeatedly.

The most relevant part of the story, however, is that despite repeated threats, the quality manager was not seriously challenged. That is the most important lesson. You and I know that we will not be beaten if we have the courage of our convictions. If we know we are right, we must preserve our integrity and stand up and be counted. Almost invariably, the opposition will back down. And if he doesn't, carry it to your boss. Let him know firmly you will not tolerate garbage being shipped. If he threatens to fire you, quit. You're going to lose your job anyway when customer dissatisfaction rises to an all-time high and quality costs double. Why lose your reputation?

That will almost never happen. Most of the time the manufacturing manager will back down. He knows you're right, but like anybody else, he's going to get every free ride he can. If you're foolish enough to let him get his way, you will be the loser and he the winner. That's the way the game is played. But if you have the courage to defend what you believe in, you will gain the respect of the organization. People will instinctively trust you, and you will have enhanced your reputation and the reputation of quality assurance.

8. A Quality Assurance Manager Only a Mother Could Love

Very often, the quality manager feels sorry for himself. The marketing people are beating him over the head to improve outgoing quality levels from the factory while the manufacturing people are eating him alive because he's "holding up shipments" during routine inspections and tests. His boss is constantly after him to reduce scrap and rework on one hand,

and coercing him to cut inspection costs 10 percent on the other hand. The general manager is insisting on number one competitive quality levels while the vice-president of finance is arbitrarily slicing his capital and expense budgets. The product engineering manager is forcing his new product through manufacturing while the manufacturing manager is angrily denouncing its state of readiness for production. Both people blame the quality manager. The city, state, and federal governments are constantly passing new laws that place restrictions on the product, and the company steadfastly challenges those changes. The person in the middle is the quality assurance manager.

Is it any wonder, then, that he feels almost psychotically singled out and pressured? It is a known fact that quality assurance—from inspector to director—is one of the highest stress-level occupations in the world today. You bet he feels sorry for himself.

The problems can be countered. With an achievable plan, a quality policy, an effective organization, and the use of other methods described in this book, the quality manager can reduce the level of stress. But make no mistake, he can never eliminate it. There will *always* be people who either cannot or will not understand and recognize the company's quality goals. The adversary system precludes 100-percent recognition.

When departments have different organizational imperatives—and they all do—the condition of battle among departments will exist. The best the quality manager can hope for is for other department managers to understand and be willing to accept the importance of the role played by quality. However, you can be sure that they will not allow that understanding and willingness to interfere substantially with their departmental goals.

The production control manager, for example, may be

sympathetic toward quality goals, but when the crunch comes and he must choose between high quality and meeting delivery dates, delivery dates will win out every time.

For that reason, many quality managers I have known have looked at quality with the fervor of a missionary. Quality in their eyes has become something greater than the cold, impersonal objective contained in a business plan. It has become almost a religion in itself, and many quality managers have pursued their goals with fanatical zeal.

Unfortunately, the natives usually resist the missionary, and even if they become somewhat frightened of his dedication, they will not abandon their ways. So the quality missionary may fail in his mission if he takes this emotional approach. Dedication to one's job is important. But in the business world that dedication must be matched by objectivity. The quality manager has been and will continue to be assaulted on all sides, but he must constantly hold to his plans and he must pursue them in a forthright and objective manner.

Chapter VI

A Final Test of Your Skills

My interest is in the future because I am going to spend the rest of my life there.

—CHARLES F. KETTERING

1. How Good Is Your Qualitysense Now?

The ultimate test of your qualitysense rests with your ability to improve your company's quality levels and reduce its quality costs. This book has developed an approach that has never been discussed quite this way before in print.

Yet many quality professionals today, including executives and managers of other functional disciplines, have been very successful in applying the principles outlined in this book. Chapter III, for example, has formed the nucleus of many a company's quality system.

Let's see how well you've done your homework. This is your final exam. If you miss any of the questions, return to the appropriate sections for further study. Be warned, however, that a few of the questions (like many quality problems) are not what they appear to be at first glance.

I am sure that you now realize it is your professionalism that sets the stage for the effectiveness of your company's quality program. Its success or failure begins in your office, at your desk. Your attitude toward quality, your perception of its role, your understanding of its function—all of these and more—shape the quality program and determine its eventual outcome.

If you know what to do and how to do it, everything will turn out fine. Your quality effort will be a success. If you don't know what to do, however, quality will most probably suffer, and you will lose customers, increase costs, and get in trouble with any number of the governmental regulatory agencies that audit your business and your product.

Let's see just how much you really have learned about

quality. The following multiple choice questions will test your ability to determine the essential differences between a successful quality program and an outright failure. The corrects answers follow the test.

1. Poor quality is most often the result of:
   (a) Ineffective quality assurance people
   (b) Unmotivated production operators
   (c) The union
   (d) Top management inattention
   (e) Old machine tools, poor design, and faulty customer service
   (f) All of the above
   (g) None of the above
2. Quality assurance should report to:
   (a) Manufacturing
   (b) Engineering
   (c) Marketing
   (d) Chief executive officer
   (e) Finance
   (f) Personnel
   (g) None of the above
3. Product quality procedures should be applied to:
   (a) Manufacturing
   (b) Manufacturing and engineering
   (c) Engineering
   (d) All company functions
   (e) Marketing
   (f) Functions determined to be appropriate by the president
4. The objective of a quality program is to:
   (a) Reduce scrap, rework, and sorting costs
   (b) Reduce warranty costs and customer complaints
   (c) Both (a) and (b)
   (d) Make all people in the company quality conscious

    (e) Increase return on investment
    (f) All of the above
5. When severe quality problems permeate the organization, the most productive approach is to:
    (a) Provide more money to combat quality problems
    (b) Reorganize the quality assurance department
    (c) Hire a new quality assurance manager or contract a consultant to analyze needs
    (d) Increase the inspection force
    (e) Appoint a task force to study the problem
    (f) None of the above
6. Your new quality assurance manager should have an in-depth background in:
    (a) Quality assurance work
    (b) Statistics
    (c) Engineering
    (d) Manufacturing, with an emphasis on quality assurance
    (e) None of the above
7. Quality is the direct responsibility of:
    (a) Quality assurance
    (b) Manufacturing, engineering, and marketing
    (c) The president
    (d) All of the above
8. A successful quality program is the result of:
    (a) A dynamic quality assurance department
    (b) Top management commitment
    (c) An aggressive plan of action for quality improvement
    (d) All of the above

Test Answers

1. If you read the book carefully, this answer will be apparent. Poor quality is almost always tied to the indifference

or inattentiveness of top management. The correct answer, therefore, is (d). Although ineffective quality people and unmotivated production operators can, and do, cause poor quality, they are almost always ineffective and unmotivated because a top management team did not provide the attention needed to mount an effective attack on quality problems. Inevitably, this lack of attention results in lackadaisical quality performance throughout the entire company. The same logic applies to old machine tools, poor design, and faulty customer service.

Blaming the unions, on the other hand, is ridiculous. The point has already been made about the strong German unions whose members produce top-quality products.

2. This should come as no surprise. The proper answer is (g), as you have learned from Chapter III, Section 2, "To Whom Should Quality Assurance Report?" The answer does not lie in manufacturing, engineering, or marketing. Neither should quality assurance report to personnel or finance. That arrangement would be organizationally ruinous. Neither personnel nor finance has the faintest organizational relationship with quality assurance; and since they are both specialized staff services, as is quality assurance, one person wouldn't have enough specialized knowledge in both areas to do both of them justice.

The closest answer, other than (g), is the chief executive officer. Actually, quality assurance should almost always report directly to the first level of general management, whether that person's title is general manager or president. The quality function would then be on an organizational step equal to that of the other functional and staff services of the company.

3. At first glance, the right answer may appear to be (f). Unfortunately, the president may not have enough insight into the quality function to say what's important and what

isn't. The best answer is (d). After all, isn't the maintenance manual for the product just as important as the product itself? If critical portions of the manual are wrong, the product will suffer, and the customer will be just as unhappy as if the product failed when he first received it.

Quality doesn't relate to manufacturing alone. It must be inherent in the design, in the service, and in all support functions needed to conduct the affairs of the business. The section on the quality assurance credo explained the need for productive quality practices in different functions of the business.

4. Although the ancillary, or supporting, objectives of the quality program may be to reduce scrap, rework, sorting, and warranty costs, the true objective is to increase return on investment. Therefore, (e) is the correct answer. All company functions are aimed at ROI, and quality is no exception. The valuable contributions quality can make to ROI, however, have not generally been understood or appreciated by the executive suite. Neither have they been exploited by most quality managers, because the focus of the managers has been on technical excellence. This book shows executives and managers alike how to shift that focus to ROI.

5. Typically, when most companies face severe quality problems, their response has been to reorganize the quality function, pump money into more testing equipment, increase inspection forces (normally a totally worthless move), or appoint a task force to study the problem and recommend solutions.

None of these moves strikes at the root cause of the problem. Unless the problems are known it is usually wasteful to reorganize or to commit additional resources. They may miss the target completely.

Neither is an internal task force the answer. Generally, it will be staffed by the very same people who got you into this mess to begin with. Their solutions are liable to compound the problem.

The best response is (c). Hire a new quality manager or contract a consultant to analyze needs. An outsider, if he knows his business, will analyze the problems without prejudice and normally arrive at the most productive and useful solutions.

6. Most quality managers are recruited from the technical ranks and, accordingly, have a strong technical orientation. But, as we have read in "The Quasar Humiliation," a technical orientation may not only be inadequate, it may actually hinder the quality manager's chances for success. Therefore, a strong technical background in statistics or engineering may not be the best preparatory background for an individual aspiring to be a quality manager.

That same logic applies to the quality manager plucked from the ranks of the quality assurance department, particularly if his whole career has been within the confines of that speciality. His very immersion in what most probably has been a technically oriented quality function subjects him to the same misconceptions shared by the quality manager fresh from the product engineering environment.

The best bet is to recruit a person with sufficient depth in quality assurance who has also had the advantage of working in another environment, where he has learned to utilize those resources at his command efficiently. A manufacturing background, for example, is ideal. The new man would then be in a position to understand how quality relates to other functions, and would be able to ply his trade in the best possible manner for the betterment of the company. He would, in other words, have a broad-based business outlook. Answer (d) fits that requirement.

7. Quality is the responsibility of those who design the product, manufacture it, sell it, and service it. The most ap-

propriate answer is (b). Quality assurance, on the other hand, has the responsibility to make sure that those functional areas are doing the right things to make quality happen, to set the stage to make people aware of the ramifications of quality, and to trace the progress of the quality program. But it *cannot* do the jobs themselves. Those are properly the responsibility of manufacturing, engineering, and marketing.

Although the president has the job of providing the right environment to allow quality to flourish, he is not *directly* responsible for quality. Only the functional areas can make things happen on a day-in, day-out basis to get the quality job done. The distinction is not always obvious, but it is always there.

8. A successful quality program is always the result of top management commitment, a dynamic quality control department, and an aggressive plan of action for quality improvement that involves the people in engineering, marketing, and manufacturing. The correct answer to this question is (d).

A successful quality program commits all levels of the organization and provides them with an understanding of the impact of quality as well as the tools with which to make things happen.

2. The Road Ahead

It is difficult for me to visualize a scenario in which the importance of quality to consumers declines. Depression or prosperity, quality will make gains for three basic reasons.

First, consumers expect more today, and their increasing knowledge and sophistication will be a continuing force behind that impetus. Only in a robotized, 1984-type of society—or in a world devastated by war—can that trend be reversed. Excluding those two terrible possibilities, companies supplying products and services will need to upgrade their quality systems and programs continually to reach and satisfy more demanding customers. That trend will be accentuated as prosperity continues because consumers will be making free choices for goods and services among increasing numbers of competitive products.

Second, as long as there are people, there will be governments, and as societies mature governments must play a more active role. We are confronted today with an almost staggering multitude of laws and regulations, all of which demand heightened quality efforts just to keep pace with the new laws. The public may revolt against continued governmental interference, but government will always be with us to a large extent, and its role in public safety and in quality will only intensify, never abate.

Third, quality is the last accessible frontier for cost reduction. Although company forms and functions may change drastically in the future, those changes are essentially evolutionary. The pressures for impacting ROI with workable cost reduction efforts, however, are intense right now and quality costs are the last costs to be addressed under known management techniques. More and more companies will be turning to quality professionals to help them with those efforts.

The true quality professionals, then, will have greater opportunities to make substantial contributions to their companies and to the public than the quality professionals of yesterday. Their influence on the economic scene will be felt for generations to come.

Index